Holy Laughter and The Toronto Blessing

Holy Laughter and The Toronto Blessing

An Investigative Report

James A. Beverley

ZondervanPublishingHouse
Grand Rapids, Michigan

A Division of HarperCollinsPublishers

Holy Laughter and The Toronto Blessing
Copyright © 1995 by James A. Beverley

Requests for information should be addressed to:

📖 Zondervan Publishing House
Grand Rapids, Michigan 49530

ISBN: 0-310-20497-6

Edited by Verlyn D. Verbrugge
Interior design by Joe Vriend

Printed in the United States of America

96 97 98 99 00 01 02 /❖ DH/ 10 9 8 7 6 5 4 3

Contents

To my wonderful wife
Gloria
and our terrific children
Andrea and Derek
with much love and admiration

Preface

In March of 1995, Peter Jennings, anchor for ABC News, did a special documentary entitled "In the Name of God." The hour-long feature explored, with a great deal of sympathy, three of the more fascinating stories of modern-day religion: the seeker-sensitive church, the Vineyard movement, and the Holy Laughter revival associated with South African evangelist Rodney Howard-Browne, the popular and controversial minister who refers to himself as "The Holy Ghost Bartender."

This book deals with the latter two topics and attempts to provide for the larger Christian and secular world the results of my investigative report on Holy Laughter and The Toronto Blessing. Over a year ago, word was starting to spread worldwide about an unusual renewal that began on January 20, 1994, at the Airport Vineyard, then located just west of Toronto's Pearson International Airport. The roots of The Toronto Blessing lie, at least in part, in the ministry of Rodney Howard-Browne. This explains the focus in this report both on the Vineyard movement and on Howard-Browne.

My study of the Vineyard goes back to 1991, when I was asked to write on this popular charismatic movement for *The Canadian Baptist*, my denominational magazine. That article probed in depth the conflicts over John Wimber's relationship with the Kansas City prophets. Since that time, I have continued to monitor developments in the Vineyard and in the modern prophecy movement.

In the fall of 1994, Mickey Maudlin, managing editor of *Christianity Today*, asked me to do an article on the issues raised by the renewal at the Airport Vineyard. From my initial work for that article, I realized that a book-length study was in order. I believed that my long-term study of the Vineyard equipped me to provide some objective analysis of the heated debate both about The Toronto Blessing and Rodney Howard-Browne.

There seems to be no limit to the invective and insults traded by opposing forces in the debate about the Vineyard movement and Howard-Browne. Given this, it would be naive to think my book will bring approval from all quarters. However, I have written with optimism that my analysis will be redemptive and helpful to those who seek guidance through the maze of issues that emerge in responding to Holy Laughter and The Toronto Blessing.

I invite my readers to interact with my research with openness and good faith. I have tried hard to keep that same spirit in focus in my dialogues (through conversation and/or study) with John Wimber, Rodney Howard-Browne, Todd Hunter, Kenn Gulliksen, John Arnott, Paul Cain, Mike Bickle, Randy Clark, Guy Chevreau, Jack Deere, Hank Hanegraaff, Tom Stipe, John MacArthur, and Warren Smith—just to mention a few of the key voices in the debate. Even when I am critical of specific positions, I have tried my best to avoid questioning the motives and integrity of others.

No book is written in isolation, and thus some words of appreciation are in order. First, I am grateful to Stan Gundry, editor in chief at ZondervanPublishingHouse, for his instant enthusiasm for my book proposal. Thanks also to Ed van der Maas, senior acquisitions editor, for his encouragement, and to Verlyn Verbrugge, senior editor, for the immense work he did in moving this book along to final printing. I also want to acknowledge the creative work of Paula Gibson on the book cover.

This book was written in the middle of regular academic life, and I owe much to my students at Ontario Theological Seminary. They encouraged me by their patience and input on various themes covered in the book. My colleagues on faculty have also endured my endless talk about my ongoing investigation. I am grateful for advice and encouragement from Nelson Annan, Brian Cunnington, Grant Gordon, John Kessler, Don Leggett, Roy Matheson, Steve Roy, Victor Shepherd, David Sherbino, Irving Whitt, and John Vissers.

Three faculty members were especially supportive during my long sieges of study. Kevin Quast, professor of New Testament, brought great help to me through his friendship and through his answers to my endless questions about my computer problems. John Wilkinson, Professor of Youth and Family Ministries, kept me energized by constant words of support and encouragement to stick with the task. Finally, my boss, Ian Rennie, academic dean, offered me the triple resource of his learning in church history, his longing for God's renewing work in the church today, and his open spirit to Christians from all backgrounds.

I am also deeply grateful to staff at Ontario Theological Seminary, who have helped me in various ways. Bonnie Rowe and Sharolyn McLeod provided crucial help at specific points, Sue Regier and Annie McKeown spent endless hours in typing, copying, faxing, and a whole multitude of other tasks that form the backdrop to the research and writing of this book.

I have had conversations with hundreds of people over the last four years about the Vineyard movement. More recently, I have had further rounds of conversations about The Toronto Blessing and Rodney Howard-Browne. I am grateful for everyone who gave me their time and ideas for my consideration. Several people have been especially helpful in my ongoing research. Bob Hunter and Wayne Sproule helped immensely on resources for study. Pat Minichello came to my aid when I visited Long Island. Clark Pinnock was, as always, a source of inspiration. Don Goertz gave me historical advice about interpreting Jonathan Edwards. I also turned to Jarold K. Zeman, my earliest mentor in theology, for his wise and thoughtful counsel. David Harrell Jr. helped in analyzing Paul Cain and the healing renewals of the 1950s. I am grateful to Dr. John Axler and Dr. Sharon Cohen for their help on medical investigation of healing claims.

Many Vineyard and ex-Vineyard pastors and other Christian leaders and scholars have also endured my repeated requests for information. I appreciate especially the kindness extended to me by John Arnold, Bette Borghi, Mike Bickle, Ken Blue, Blaine Cook, Ernie Gruen, Kenn Gulliksen, Kim Hutchins, Todd Hunter, Jeff Kirby, George Mallone, Kevin Springer, Tom and Mary Ellen Stipe, and Sandy Younger. I appreciate Hank Hanegraaff for his friendship, openness, and support in my probing of his views on the Vineyard and the Word Faith movement. Rodney Howard-Browne was generous with time and conversation at meetings in Long Island, New York, and in subsequent phone calls. Over several years, John Wimber has been gracious in his response to my in-depth probing of the movement he leads.

Since my earliest study of the Vineyard, it has been a privilege to learn from Sam Thompson, former National Coordinator of the Association of Vineyard Churches. Sam has been a model to me of Christian love and goodwill, characteristics that he has modeled in his continuing reflections about his many years of work side by side with John Wimber.

Larry Matthews, the editor of *The Canadian Baptist* and a long-time friend, has been there for me in my various projects, and I am thankful for his support and encouragement. As always, my twin brother, Bob Beverley, came through with deep and penetrating reflections for me to consider. He also joined me for my interview with Rodney Howard-Browne and helped me to process that interesting visit. My dad, George Beverley, inspires me with his love and encouragement and his own strong faith in the gospel.

Finally, and most important, I owe an enormous debt to my wonderful wife, Gloria, and to our two children, Andrea and Derek. They supported me the best by enduring the most. Just after completing the defense of my Ph.D. thesis on the Unification Church (Fall, 1994), I began working on the article for *Christianity Today* and then turned to the larger task of working on this book. For months my wife and children have given their love and patience to me as I concentrated on the study of Holy Laughter and The Toronto Blessing. They have put up with my late nights, weekend work, and false prophecies of when the book would be done. I am grateful for their faith in this project and, most important, for their willingness to support me by all that it means to be a family.

James A. Beverley
Toronto, Ontario
May 1995

One

The Holy Spirit Has Landed

In the London newspaper the *Sunday Telegraph* of June 19, 1994, its several million readers were told that "British Airways flight 092 took off from Toronto Airport on Thursday evening just as the Holy Spirit was landing on a small building 100 yards from the end of the runway." This widely-circulated quotation refers to what has become known around the world as "The Toronto Blessing." This is an apt description of the way millions of Christians now regard the ministry connected with the Airport Vineyard in Toronto. There is widespread belief throughout the charismatic and Pentecostal world that something powerful and amazing is happening in one of Canada's leading cities. Marc Dupont, the prophet of the Airport Vineyard, has suggested that Toronto may have been the choice for this latest renewal of the Holy Spirit because of its cosmopolitan significance. One study suggests that Toronto is the most ethnically diverse city on this planet. Thus, just as Pentecost initiated the renewal of the church to the diverse nations of the world in the first century, so The Toronto Blessing is bringing renewal to a vast number of nations and peoples in the last years of the twentieth century.

Regardless of what one may think of the claim that the Holy Spirit lands regularly at the Airport Vineyard near Toronto's Pearson International Airport, there is no doubt that The Toronto Blessing represents one of the most interesting and amazing stories in recent years. Since January 20, 1994, there have been meetings at the Airport Vineyard every night of the week except Monday. Several different airlines offer a discount to people who fly to Toronto to attend the evening worship services. Major hotels in the west end of the city provide discounts to those who want to be in the city for The Toronto Blessing. Already four books have been published on the topic, in addition to hundreds of articles and magazine stories. This amazing story has also been covered by Canadian, American, and international television crews.

It is also well known that The Toronto Blessing has not received a favorable review from all Christians. Controversy has surfaced in individual churches and throughout entire denominations. As will be explained later, some severe allegations have been leveled against the basic integrity of this latest phase of the Vineyard. Much of that controversy has centered around the strange manifestations that have taken place in the nightly meetings. Two chapters in this book will deal in detail with this aspect of The Toronto Blessing.

Journalist Robert Hough did a story on the Airport Vineyard for *Toronto Life Magazine*. His account gives a picture of part of an evening meeting:

> The man sitting beside me, Dwayne from California, roared like a wounded lion. The woman beside Dwayne started jerking so badly her hands struck her face. People fell like dominoes, collapsing chairs as they plunged to the carpeting. They howled like wolves, brayed like donkeys and—in the case of a young man standing near the sound board—started clucking like a feral chicken. And the tears! Never have I seen people weep so hysterically, as though every hurt they'd ever encountered had risen to the surface and popped like an overheated tar bubble. This was eerie . . . stuff—people were screaming, their bodies jerking unnaturally, their faced contorted with tics.[1]

Despite these strange manifestations, there has been no hesitation on the part of many Christians around the world to engage in similar behavior. Writing in *Christian Research Journal*, Paul Carden noted the influence of The Toronto Blessing in England: "An epidemic of laughter is spreading across the land, flashing like lightning from church to church. It is the most bizarre thing to happen in the religious life of Britain for some time. Is it a case of 'whom the god's wish to destroy they first make mad'?"[2] Carden's suggestion that Christians may be going mad would be readily and strongly denounced by millions in favor of The Toronto Blessing. They would reply, as Jonathan Edwards did in his day, that this madness has brought great and wonderful renewal to the Christian church throughout the world.

Roots of The Toronto Blessing

When Christians today think about the outpouring of the Holy Spirit at Pentecost, they agree that this renewal was fundamentally divine in origin. However, even at Pentecost human factors were at work. After all, human beings were the ones who had gathered in the Upper Room on that day. These same people had been disciples of Jesus Christ, and their anointing by the Holy Spirit was preceded by their time with Jesus and his ministry on earth. In the most fundamental sense, then, Pentecost is rooted in the human ministry of the Son of God.

In a similar vein, even the most ardent supporters of The Toronto Blessing realize a human factor is involved in the origin and spread of the fires connected with the Airport Vineyard. The roots of this renewal lie first of all in the ministry of John Wimber, the international leader of the Vineyard. Todd Hunter, now National Coordinator of Vineyard Churches, believes that it is Wimber's international reputation that set the stage for people being willing to come to Vineyard meetings in Toronto.

One of the other major leaders behind The Toronto Blessing is Rodney Howard-Browne. Known as the laughing evangelist, Howard-Browne is from South Africa, but felt the call of God to come to America in 1987. (In a later chapter of this book, we will explore his specific ministry and teaching.) He has played a central role in the origin of The Toronto Blessing. He believes that God has given him a special anointing to renew the church with the power of the Holy Spirit. He actually refers to himself as "The Holy Ghost

Bartender," in light of his claim that he is giving to the church the "new wine" of the Holy Spirit.

Randy Clark, a Vineyard pastor from St. Louis, heard about Howard-Browne's incredible impact on some of his friends. So he went to hear Howard-Browne at a revival meeting in Tulsa, Oklahoma. While there, he received the laying on of hands from Rodney Howard-Browne, which brought to Randy a powerful renewal, including the manifestation of Holy Laughter.

In the fall of 1993, John Arnott, the senior pastor of the Toronto Airport Vineyard, was influenced by several people talking about the renewal of the church through Holy Laughter. Arnott had been anointed by the Pentecostal Claudio Freidzon, and he was also greatly impressed by the testimony of Randy Clark about his personal renewal. As a result, he invited Clark to preach at the Airport Vineyard on January 20, 1994. Much to Arnott's and Clark's surprise, there was a sudden outpouring of the Holy Spirit that evening. Shortly thereafter a decision was made to extend the renewal to nightly meetings, so that there could be greater participation from other Christians who needed a touch from God.

A Typical Evening Service

Since some of the distortions about The Toronto Blessing are based on inadequate information about what actually happens in Toronto, it is necessary from the outset to get a glimpse of what a typical evening service is like. The shape of these meetings fell into a standard pattern rather early in the renewal, though there is certainly variety, depending on who leads worship and who preaches. Nevertheless, there are four phases of a typical nightly meeting.

(1) The service begins with an hour or more of chorus singing. This praise and worship time is led by a worship team under the supervision of Jeremy Sinnott, whose background is in the Fellowship of Evangelical Baptist Churches, one of the larger Baptist groups in Canada. During this hour there may be an occasional hymn. Even during the singing there will be various manifestations or examples of ecstatic behavior. Hundreds of people will lift up

their hands in praise to God, while others will dance. There may also be rounds of Holy Laughter or other more unusual manifestations, such as shaking, roaring like a lion, or loud shouting and screaming.

(2) The next phase of worship consists of testimony time. John Arnott or other Vineyard leaders invite people to the front to share what God has been doing in their lives. The testimony time is often the most dramatic moment in worship, since people recount powerful stories of renewal, healing, and conversion. During the reporting of the testimony, the specific individual may manifest certain signs, and usually at the end of their testimony, they are asked if they want to receive more from the Holy Spirit. The Vineyard leaders then pray for the person, who is often then "slain in the Spirit."

(3) The third component of a typical evening celebration is the preaching time, which can last anywhere from twenty minutes to an hour. About five times in the first year of the renewal, the preaching was stopped abruptly; on a couple other occasions there was no preaching at all. Sometimes the preaching is drowned out by the sounds of Holy Laughter, though this is not the usual occurrence. The quality of preaching varies, depending on the speaker, the individual's style of delivery, and the extent of focus on the biblical text. By and large, the messages focus on spiritual renewal, and they often involve lengthy storytelling and accounts of how the renewal is spreading to other parts of the world.

(4) The first three phases of worship normally take up to two and a half hours. At the end of the sermon an invitation is given for personal salvation, followed by the general invitation to experience the renewing touch of the Holy Spirit. At this point, people are invited to come forward to receive ministry time, or they may be asked to go to other parts of the church to wait for ministry team members to anoint them and pray for them. This last part of the evening meeting is the longest part. Usually it begins about 10:00 P.M. and can last from two to four hours, though it usually does not go much later than 12:30 or 1:00 A.M.

People are regularly told not to receive prayer from just anyone. This rule came about because there were several incidents where people came to the evening worship and took it upon themselves to pray for others without the consent of the Vineyard leadership. Sometimes the prayers offered were inappropriate, other times there were false prophetic words given to individuals, and a few times there were accounts of inappropriate touching of others. In light of these problems, the Vineyard leadership instituted a policy of having the recognized ministry team members wear special badges, and they advise people in the congregation not to receive prayer from an unauthorized person. There have actually been a couple of reports of people from witchcraft groups infiltrating these meetings, though these have not been substantiated.

Since the ministry time is obviously the most controversial aspect of the Toronto Vineyard meetings, a further word is in order about describing what occurs. Most people on a given night go forward to receive prayer. They are asked to stand in orderly fashion and to wait for someone to come to them. Occasionally people display Spirit manifestations before someone prays for them, though usually the manifestations accompany or follow prayer from someone on the ministry team. It would be wrong to say that the ministry time—or, as it is often referred to, "carpet time"—involves complete disorder. But it would also be wrong to imply that this phase of worship amounts to what you would see at a typical non-charismatic church! In fact, even many Pentecostals find their perspectives stretched as they attend Vineyard meetings and see different manifestations displayed during carpet time.

Snapshots of The Toronto Blessing

Since I live in Toronto and have had the opportunity to attend many Vineyard meetings, I thought it would be appropriate to give some indication of the range of realities faced in The Toronto Blessing. I will provide a panoramic picture of various scenes from my own involvement, in order to give some insight into the movement for those unable to attend the Airport Vineyard. I am fully aware that I write as an outsider and that one gets a different set of pictures by reading Guy Chevreau's *Catch the Fire* or Dave Roberts' *The Toronto Blessing*. However, I think the following selection of snapshots represents a balanced picture of what it is like to investigate and address this famous renewal.

One night in June, 1994, I was sitting on the platform at the original Airport Vineyard site talking with John Wimber. I asked him if the phenomena that went on in the evening worship were new to him. "Not at all," he replied. "I have seen everything before in other Vineyard services around the world."

One afternoon I was out at the Airport Vineyard to do an interview with John Arnott. As I walked into the main sanctuary of the church, I noticed a group of teenagers over in the corner praying together. It occurred to me that whatever criticisms one might have of The Toronto Blessing, the fact that teenagers were gathered together during their school break for prayer indicated that something was right about this renewal.

Another evening I took my son, Derek, to a worship service with me. When a friend of mine asked me if I would like to have prayer, Derek simply took the question to mean whether or not I would agree to have this friend pray for me in his devotions at a later time. When Derek discovered that I was going to stand for prayer right at that moment, he was scared that I was going to fall over or act like an animal. Later my son told me that the "catcher" behind me was blowing on my shirt.

On another occasion, late during the ministry time, I noticed a man and two women reaching out and touching one another with fresh jolts of "Spirit-power." Every touch of hands increased the laughter and spasms in their bodies. Finally, in what is viewed as a great outburst of Spirit-power, the man fell off his chair, and his head hit the concrete with a loud thud. It did not seem to bother him, however, for he continued laughing.

I traveled to Oakville to visit Guy Chevreau. Guy and I had spent time together in doctoral work at the Toronto School of Theology. I was excited to hear about the tremendous personal renewal that has come to him and his wife, Janis. Though I disagree with some of the arguments in his book *Catch the Fire*, The Toronto Blessing has been strengthened by the intellectual leadership he has brought to the teaching ministry of the Airport Vineyard.

The Airport Vineyard has struggles like any church. Several members have talked to me about some serious hurts they have experienced when they were dealt with rather abruptly and without due process. The differences and issues were not handled carefully in love.

At one meeting I went to the front to say hello to Mike Bickle, a Vineyard pastor from Kansas City. He gave me a hug, and we talked for a few minutes. When I tried to work my way back to be with my wife and friends, there was no room to move to the other side of the large auditorium because of so many bodies in front of me. The only possible route was to go in front of a woman waving her arms wildly in a forward direction. I could be in danger of getting hurt if I stepped in her path. It then occurred to me that if the Holy Spirit was behind her actions, I was in no danger, since the Holy Spirit does not desire harm for people. Furthermore, Christian patterns of behavior indicate that we do not hurt our fellow human beings. So I moved in faith in front of the woman and said, "Excuse me," and her arms shifted the other direction to allow me to pass!

On the first anniversary of The Toronto Blessing, the service lasted until about 2:30 A.M.. At 1:45 A.M., one of the Vineyard ministry team members came over to me and said that Randy Clark would be willing to give me an interview. He was able to get away from the crowds at about 2:30 A.M. Even later in the hotel lobby people came up to him to ask for prayer. He mentioned to me the next night that the mission impulse out of the The Toronto Blessing would be enormous.

Word has spread throughout the Christian community in Canada that The Toronto Blessing has been endorsed by David Mainse, the host of *100 Huntley Street*, a well-known Christian television show in Canada. He spoke at the Airport Vineyard in March, 1995, and was open about his spiritual life. He is now receiving strong criticism for his support of this renewal.

One night I went to the Airport Vineyard with my daughter, Andrea. We were both astonished at one of the episodes at the evening meeting. A pastor from Oregon was pouring out his heart about his emotional and spiritual pain. Near the end of his testimony, a man in the congregation began a loud round of holy laughter. It was disheartening to see the way the Oregon pastor's testimony was drowned out by the Holy Laughter, and he was visibly hurt by the quenching of his voice.

After writing a one-page column that raised concerns about The Toronto Blessing, I was disappointed to be warned that I was on dangerous ground by daring to question this great movement of God. This brought back to my mind memories of the divine threats raised against critics of the Kansas City prophets. These kind of warnings are a signal of insecurity more than of prophetic power.

One time while participating in an afternoon worship at the Vineyard, I decided to go for prayer and anointing, believing that there would be nothing intrinsically wrong with having fellow Christians pray for me at the Airport Vineyard. However, the behavior of people around me was so wild and chaotic that I simply could not bring my mind to feel comfortable about prayer in such a context.

Another time I felt a real openness to stand in a long line and wait for prayer from John Arnott. John did not know at that time who I was, and I approached this opportunity with real openness. I asked the Holy Spirit to do whatever he wanted to do in my life. When John laid his hands on me, I felt nothing strange and experienced no manifestations. The woman beside me had been slain in the Spirit with dramatic power, and she actually reached out and grabbed my arm just as John Arnott was praying for me. I thought that maybe one of my friends had sneaked up behind me to try to give me some help in the Spirit, but it was the woman reaching out as she crashed to the floor.

One night during the ministry time a teenage girl was broken and weeping with deep passion, obviously distraught about some things in her life. She was on the floor being embraced by an older woman, who was cradling her in her arms and comforting her with the love of Jesus Christ. There are too few churches where teenagers and senior citizens embrace each other in deep moments of spiritual and emotional renewal.

The evening Mike Bickle preached, twice during his powerful sermon he had an awareness of his own sin and how deeply the church has failed in its mission of obedience to the gospel of Jesus Christ. During those two moments Mike cried publicly. This was a moving and touching moment.

On the anniversary night Randy Clark told a story about Hudson Taylor receiving a vision in the middle of a service, in which the Lord revealed to him the outbreak of the two world wars in this century. I doubted that was true, for that kind of revelation is untypical of prophetic material in the Old Testament. Later, John Arnott brought someone up from the audience who knew a lot about Hudson Taylor's life, and John asked this man to inform Randy that his story was probably inaccurate. Randy was open to the correction. John Arnott's care for the truth is admirable.

One evening when my son joined me for another meeting, we closely watched a group of teenagers under the power of the Holy Spirit. What disappointed both of us was the obviously contrived nature of their ministry time. True, not all of the teenagers are faking. However, there is a danger in the expectation that manifestations must be a regular part of a Christian's life. To watch a teenage girl stagger around with a Coke in one hand while obviously trying to imitate the adults in the service was a sad sight.

One of my friends talked with me at one of the meetings, commenting on how much he had learned from Atlantic Baptist College in Moncton, New Brunswick, where I used to teach. He was appreciative of the doctrinal and biblical learning he had gained there. However, he also told me that there was a danger in the Baptist tradition of having T-bone steak served on ice. This is obviously a provocative way of warning those of us in noncharismatic traditions that our doctrine must be matched with inner fire.

One day an informed observer mentioned to me that people come to Toronto with no money to pay for a hotel room after the nightly meeting is over. Many of these people are put up in homes of the local Vineyard members, or they choose to sleep in the church all night, sometimes in the conviction that this experience alone will bring God's power within their lives.

One of my friends told me that one evening when he was receiving prayer, much to his surprise, he was slain in the Spirit. He remembers being astounded by the power that overcame him, causing him to fall backwards on the floor. He was even worried that he had said some inappropriate words while falling to the ground. One of the reasons we should be open to the authenticity of the experience of being slain in the Spirit is that it has happened to people who do not expect it to happen and are not really eager for it to come upon them. However, as they open themselves up to pray, they believe the Holy Spirit has chosen this venue for personal and spiritual renewal.

On the first anniversary night, four thousand believers sang "Holy, Holy, Holy" in a wonderful moment of celebration and worship. Critics of The Toronto Blessing must constantly remember that it is the people of God who are coming to Toronto and are raising their voices in praise to the heavenly Father.

One night at the Vineyard, a television crew was making a documentary for European television. One of the people being interviewed was a psychologist from England who favored The Toronto Blessing. He told the television crew that he knew of no one coming to the Airport Vineyard who had a negative emotional or psychological reaction. However, there are more than a few people who have been deeply upset and wounded by some of the negative aspects of this renewal.

One of my colleagues at the Ontario Theological Seminary, where I now teach, told me of a close friend of his who, during an evening service at the Airport Vineyard, had been won back to the

Lord after a lengthy period of rebellion. This person rededicated his life to the gospel and now has a renewed call to Christian ministry.

One young woman came to my office to talk about what the meetings meant for her. She had gone to the meeting one night purely out of curiosity and was not open for prayer. However, she did receive prayer after her initial hesitation, and to her surprise she found herself laughing and then weeping in deep emotional and spiritual renewal. She reports with some surprise that she has been delivered from deep channels of fear and anxiety that had plagued her life for years.

Five Interpretations of The Toronto Blessing

Whenever I teach on a particular topic in my course work, I like to inform students of various options for interpretation. These perspectives can then be kept in mind as the evidence is weighed and various issues are settled in the process of analysis. With that in mind, I would like to close this first chapter by presenting some of the different perspectives on The Toronto Blessing.

From my reading of the immense literature on this current renewal, there appear to me to be at least five different interpretations. The two most extreme interpretations adopt an eschatological or prophetic interpretation—the one positive and the other negative. We should remember something that will be noted in the next chapter, that the middle position between extremes in not necessarily the right interpretation. In other words, truth is not always in the middle, though that often may be the case. We will consider the various perspectives from the positive to the negative.

(1) The most optimistic interpretation is the view that The Toronto Blessing represents a renewal that is prophetic in significance. This renewal is part of God's will in bringing the church to its final preparation for the return of Jesus Christ. In the March/April, 1995 issue of *Spread the Fire*, for example, it is mentioned that David Yonggi Cho, the famous Korean pastor, has prophesied that the last outpouring of the Holy Spirit before the Lord

returns will begin in Canada. This incredible statement is being used to refer to The Toronto Blessing.

(2) It is true that The Toronto Blessing is a great renewal, but it should not be interpreted as having eschatological significance in any other way than any church or any part of the body of Christ has eschatological significance in being part of the kingdom of God. According to this view, The Toronto Blessing is acknowledged primarily as a supernatural and miraculous outpouring of the Holy Spirit. In its cover story on The Toronto Blessing, for example, *Charisma* magazine alludes to this renewal as being similar in nature to the beginnings of Pentecostalism at Azusa Street in Los Angeles in 1906. Parallels have also been drawn between the renewal at the Airport Vineyard and the gift of the Holy Spirit on the day of Pentecost.

(3) A third interpretation uses the phrase "mixed blessings" to describe the Toronto renewal. Simply put, the renewal connected with Rodney Howard-Browne and the Vineyard offers a mixture of good and bad, of positive and negative. This option does not center on the obvious point that in any church there is a mixture of the flesh and Spirit. Rather, it makes a much bolder claim, that this renewal has some wonderful aspects, but it also has some dangerous and harmful aspects.

(4) In a more critical position, many believe that The Toronto Blessing is fundamentally a negative reality. This renewal is not in keeping with the authentic revivals of church history, and its weaknesses are so great that Christians worldwide must be warned against it. In other words, The Toronto Blessing is no blessing at all! Some discernment is needed to understand this position. Its advocates are not suggesting that there is nothing right about the Airport Vineyard and Rodney Howard-Browne. But they claim that their criticisms are so serious that it is not God's will for a Christian to be involved with Howard-Browne or the alleged renewal in and through the Airport Vineyard.

(5) The final interpretation is the most negative. It is rooted, like the first one, in a prophetic or eschatological understanding. Accord-

ing to those who take this view, The Toronto Blessing is part of the work of the Antichrist to bring about world apostasy and the creation of a one-world church under satanic delusion. In other words, a few critics believe that the ministry of Rodney Howard-Browne and the renewal at the Airport Vineyard is not a work of God; rather, it is a mighty delusion brought on the church to create ultimate loyalty to the evil one.

It should be obvious from the vast gulf represented between the opposing perspectives of The Toronto Blessing that it would be difficult to work through a process whereby all Christians could come to a consensus on what this renewal constitutes. However, it is a task of any analyst to pay attention to the different interpretations and to keep these in mind as the material is studied, as people are interviewed, and as all of the issues are examined in the light of the Bible.

Two
Testing the Spirits

Agreement on what constitutes valid criticism or appropriate endorsement of The Toronto Blessing requires some consensus on fundamental principles in spiritual discernment. In 1 John 4:1 Christians are told to "test the spirits to see whether they are from God." Paul commands the followers of Jesus to "test everything" and "hold on to the good" (1 Thess. 5:21).

Over many years of teaching I have developed a framework for analyzing religious claims, a road map for hunting for truth. By "truth" I do not simply mean bits of factual data that are authentic. Rather, I have in mind a bigger sense of truth, the kind Jesus meant when he said: "You will know the truth, and the truth will set you free"(John 8:32).

A number of years ago I was reading a book by historian Peter Brown in which he mentioned a quotation from the Talmud that served as a guiding light for his research and scholarship: "Every judge who judges a judgment of truth, true to the truth of the matter, causes the glory of God to dwell in Israel." That quote has become a beacon for me in my study and analysis of The Toronto Blessing.

Ten Tests for Truth

In dealing with The Toronto Blessing, some Christians have argued that this recent saga is from the realm of the demonic or that the Vineyard is a cult (or at least shows cultlike tendencies). In light of such serious allegations, we must be clear about a proper standard for judging specific religious groups and views. The following ten tests are those I have used in evaluating the Vineyard and The Toronto Blessing. You will notice that they are multifaceted in nature and that each test includes further criteria for discernment. Sometimes truth hunting is easy, and the correct view is obvious. Other times scrutiny needs to recognize complexity, and a simple answer is inappropriate.

1. **The God Test**. Does the group in question recognize the one God of the Bible as the true God, the God who is the Almighty Creator of heaven and earth, the God and Father of our Lord Jesus Christ, the God known as Father, Son, and Holy Spirit?

The Trinitarian emphasis here separates Christianity from Judaism and Islam, both of which deny the Trinity. While the term *Trinity* is not in the New Testament, we have every reason to accept that God is revealed to us as Father, Son, and Holy Spirit.

2. **The Christological Test**. Does the group in question exalt Jesus Christ as the only eternal Savior, as the only eternal Son of God? Does it look to Jesus as God's final revelation, and does it glory in the life, teaching, death, resurrection, and second coming of Jesus Christ?

More and more, Christians must stand for this high Christology. It is being attacked by New Agers, who want to distinguish Jesus from the Christ. The New Testament's relentless focus on Jesus is anathema to radical feminists, who deny Jesus as a Savior because he was a man. A high Christology also undermines the liberal pluralist agenda that all roads lead to God and that Jesus is only one Savior among many.

3. **The Biblical Test**. Does the group really follow the Bible? Do they obey the many and varied commands of Scripture and believe its clear and dominant teachings? Does the particular religion or denomination add to, take away from, distort, or ignore God's Word?

It is ironic how we each apply the Bible selectively as we test ourselves and others. For example, evangelicals would probably be alarmed if their pastor was discovered to be gay, but they would likely not be overly concerned if he showed little interest in the starving of the world.

4. **The Moral Love Test**. Does the group in question follow the high morals of the Old and New Testaments? Is love central in the group, and is it really practiced by the leaders and members? Does the particular religion have a two-pronged focus of love—loving God and loving one's neighbor?

Gordon Melton, founder of The Institute for the Study of American Religion, often tries to point out to evangelicals and fundamentalists that not having love (both for God and for humans) is the greatest heresy. Paul's teaching in 1 Corinthians 13 serves as a definitive backup for Melton's view.

5. **The Spirituality Test**. Does the group show a desire for following the Holy Spirit? Is there a desire for purity and authentic spirituality? Are there signs of legalism and shallow ritualism that pervade its ethos?

At this point, we must be cautious about judging brothers and sisters in Christ's body. Fundamentally, only God knows our hearts. In other words, we must exercise extreme caution as we seek to analyze the spirituality of others in the church.

6. **The Freedom Test**. Does the group offer real freedom to individuals? Do the religious leaders in question offer space for followers to have their own opinions and views? How do leaders come under correction and discipline?

Several popular books center on this issue of freedom. For example, Ron Enroth touched a powerful nerve in his work *Churches That Abuse*.[1] Ken Blue has a helpful book, *Healing Spiritual Abuse*,[2] which centers on "the biblical answer to the wounds of legalism."

7. **The Church Test**. Is the specific religious group in continuity with the classic Christian faith? Or is the group sectarian, rigid, and narrow? Is the movement too liberal or harmfully tolerant? Is the group committed to the foundational truth that we are saved by grace and not by our own works?

Again, care must be taken in speaking against entire church groups who confess allegiance to evangelical Christian faith, for sweeping generalizations about entire denominations are dangerous.

8. **The Social/Political Test**. Does the religion care for the social well-being of individuals and about the political needs of humanity? Are the leaders doing anything practical to address the painful realities of poverty, disease, and injustice?

Thankfully, evangelicals have abandoned the dichotomy once created between social action and evangelism. In an earlier generation justice concerns were left to the "liberal" Christians, but writers like Ron Sider have helped raise awareness of the need for evangelical Christians to be "salt to the earth."

9. **The Prophetic Test**. Have the leaders of the group been false prophets, either in the sense of false predictions or of careless prophetic dogmatism? Has the grand tradition of Isaiah and Amos been bypassed? Are there prophets in our day who have a powerful word from God?

Sadly, many Christians today neglect the Old Testament, especially the prophetic books. This neglect has created significant distortion on the topic of prophecy. Most Christians think that the Old Testament prophets were primarily foretellers of the future. This, however, was only a minor aspect of their ministry. For the most part, they pronounced the sins of God's people, announced God's wrath in the short term, and gave a promise of restoration after judgment.

10. **The Rational Test**. Does a given idea or practice seem reasonable, in keeping with the path of wisdom and truth? Are the specific claims of given groups and individuals true? Or does the group exaggerate wildly? Do leaders admit to making errors?

I agree here with John MacArthur's comments in his new work *Reckless Faith*: "Although we must reject *rationalism*, we dare not repudiate *rationality*—the right use of sanctified reason, sound logic, clear thought, and common sense."[3] Vineyard members may not like MacArthur's verdicts on Wimber and his theology, but the call MacArthur makes for Christian rationality is crucial.

Preliminary Assessment of The Toronto Blessing

With regard to the above-mentioned standards—God, Christology, the Bible, morality and love, spirituality, freedom, church, social-political issues, prophecy, and rationality—admittedly, no church or evangelical tradition honors everything represented by these lofty ideals. But such tests can serve as an initial sorting ground for further discernment and analysis.

On which issues should we give Airport Vineyard leaders every benefit of the doubt? There is no need to be hesitant about their allegiance to the God of the Scriptures. They also have a high Christology and are committed to Christian morality and love. They are in full continuity with classic Christianity and pass the church test. They are also involved in social action and care about revival.

My initial hesitations involve further probing about the biblical test, the spirituality test, the freedom test, the prophetic test, and the rational test. For clarity's sake, I am not saying that The Toronto Blessing is unbiblical, that it is cultic in its authoritarianism, that it advocates false prophecy, or that its leaders are completely irrational. Such an assessment would be too strong and too one-sided. My concerns are more nuanced, especially about the biblical test and the freedom test. For example, while John Arnott and other Airport Vineyard leaders are committed to the authority of the Bible, some questions surface about their biblical emphasis and about proper interpretation of Scripture.

On the issue of spirituality, the Vineyard leaders clearly want the blessing of the Holy Spirit. However, there are some serious issues to be explored concerning the controversial and well-known manifestations associated with the movement. Furthermore, the Airport Vineyard has duplicated some common errors about the Spirit-filled life that have been made by their Pentecostal and charismatic cousins.

Likewise, I think there has been a tendency in the Vineyard to be too uncritical about leadership. John Wimber has been placed on a pedestal by some of his followers. Furthermore, The Toronto Blessing has produced such a focus on Airport Vineyard leaders that

I believe some authoritarianism manifests itself in response to criticism, even to individuals in their local fellowship.

The prophetic component of The Toronto Blessing is risky business—a topic that will be explored in chapters 9 and 10. The issues involved cannot be resolved by simply announcing whether one endorses or rejects the gift of prophecy. This modern-day controversy is too complicated to resolve so easily.

Moreover, there is an anti-intellectual spirit to The Toronto Blessing that deserves correction from John Wimber and John Arnott. When Paul writes in 1 Corinthians 1:20—"Has not God made foolish the wisdom of the world?"— he is talking about the wisdom of unregenerate, blind people, those who do not know Jesus. This verse should not be used as a weapon against Christians who have questions about certain aspects of the Airport Vineyard.

How to Study The Toronto Blessing

Given my belief that Christians have every right to study The Toronto Blessing, let me suggest further guidelines that have influenced my analysis. (1) As the above tests for truth imply, Christians should have a proper understanding of the basics, or *essentials*, of the Christian faith to bring to any study. This will provide a framework for analyzing competing truth claims and different religious practices.

(2) In every controversy, analysis must be done with a considerable degree of *patience*. We should take our time to study complex and important issues. Sometimes urgency demands a rush to judgment, particularly if the core of the Gospel is being denied. Many times, however, a hasty blessing or critique leads to error and imbalance in judgment.

(3) Analysis of The Toronto Blessing must be done in fundamental *fairness*, lest one break the command not to give "false testimony against your neighbor" (Ex. 20:16). This applies to both critics and defenders of this alleged outpouring of the Spirit.

This point is important. Selective evidence is often used in the heat of debate. For example, I could tell you that one man at the

Airport Vineyard was acting like a dog one night. It has been widely reported that Christians have been barking like dogs at various services in both Toronto and London, allegedly in duplication of similar manifestation at a revival in Kentucky in the last century. However, this man was not only barking like a dog, but he also lifted up one leg and pretended to urinate on, I guess, an invisible fire hydrant. Now, I have no doubt that this incident occurred, for it was reported to me by two men sympathetic to The Toronto Blessing. However, to be fair, I must add something as I recount this incident. I told John Arnott about it, and he was quite properly upset that someone would do such a disgusting thing. He wished that loving discipline could have been brought to the individual in question.

(4) The analysis of The Toronto Blessing must be *multifaceted*, showing an appreciation for the wide range of issues at stake in this renewal. Given the number of people who have experienced this Blessing and given the host of doctrines raised by the debate, no one comment can settle the discussion. The checklist for truth and righteousness needs to be broad, diverse, and attentive to many realities.

(5) A proper study of The Toronto Blessing will also *recognize complexity*. There are intellectual, spiritual, and psychological issues that are complicated and cannot receive quick or hasty verdicts. Experts need to be consulted on different aspects. For example, both critics and proponents cite Jonathan Edwards as an ally. This demands a thorough study of the "real" Edwards.

(6) An adequate study of The Toronto Blessing also involves the *careful analysis of hidden presuppositions*, or assumed truths, that lie behind various perspectives in this controversy. For example, the view that certain gifts of the Holy Spirit are not for today predetermines a lack of openness toward the meetings at the Airport Vineyard.

How to Think and Reason Correctly

In any controversy, truth often gets lost in the heat of the debate. For that reason, Christians should understand how to think clearly and correctly. This involves some acquaintance with what is called "informal logic." These principles of thought will help us in sorting through the various aspects of this current conflict.

- **Emotion does not settle truth.** Just because someone is heated in his or her rhetoric for or against the Airport Vineyard does not mean that view is correct. Truth is not determined by who shouts the loudest.

- **Tradition is not always right.** Opposition to this alleged new work of the Spirit is not right simply because a denomination has always stood against such things.

- **Do not give human authority figures uncritical allegiance.** Although John Wimber has endorsed the renewal in Toronto, this does not mean it must be from God. John Wimber himself could be wrong; he is not infallible. Likewise, John MacArthur, though a famous preacher, could be wrong in his opposition to the movement.

- **Be careful in your use of words.** In an article on "Ten Myths About The Toronto Blessing," I wrote that "attacks on John Wimber's theology are half-baked and careless." I should have said, for the sake of precision and truth, that "many attacks" are faulty. The way the sentence read in the article implied that no one has written a fair and accurate critique.

- **Do not force people into limited or false options.** There is no reason to think that the manifestations are either totally demonic or totally from heaven. There are other legitimate options worth exploration.

- **Do not use name-calling and put-downs as a debate tactic.** We should resist the temptation to dismiss Vineyard people as emotional basket cases. On the other side, Vineyard defenders should do better than just calling critics a group of Pharisees. This name-calling is called *argumentum ad hominem* in logic.

- **Be careful of sloppy accusations based on the presumed origin of a given idea or practice.** This principle, known as the "genetic fallacy," is a bit complicated. It is true that if the ultimate root of a teaching is from Satan, then the teaching is wrong. However, some critics look for any hint of error in the roots of The Toronto Blessing in order to dismiss the entire thing. That is unfair.

- **The popularity of something does not make it right.** The fact that thousands have come to Toronto to experience the Blessing does not automatically authenticate it. A large number of sincere Christians could indeed make mistakes in judgment.

- **The unpopularity of something does not make a judgment correct.** Again, truth cannot be settled by numbers. A lone prophet warning against The Toronto Blessing might be right, but not simply because he or she is alone.

- **The fact that something is an old or a new idea does not automatically make it right.** This is called "chronological snobbery." Some seem to think that simply because several Christians barked like dogs in the Cane Ridge revival in Kentucky a century ago means that it is right in Toronto today. But that is assuming that it was right to bark like a dog in worship on that earlier occasion.

- **Be careful in the use of "guilt by association."** This rule needs sensitive handling since certain associations can place us in sin and danger. But there are also contacts that are not intrinsically wrong. After all, Jesus was "a friend of tax collectors and sinners"(Matt. 11:19).

- **Do not dismiss good ideas or practices by letting your imagination take them to extremes.** This is known as *reductio ad absurdam*. While John Wimber teaches that Christians should pray for healing, it is unfair to argue that he does not care about proper medical care since he believes in divine healing.

- **Be prudent when using the "slippery slide" argument.** This is a popular tactic among conservative Christians. If we cannot prove something wrong in itself, we may say that it will lead to something else that is wrong. However, not all slides are slippery. For example, praying for the Holy Spirit at the Airport Vineyard does not mean that Christians are opening themselves up to anything in the demonic spirit realm.

- **Be cautious about cause and effect observations.** Consider the mother who knows that Johnny ate a chocolate bar before supper. When Johnny does not eat his lima beans at mealtime, his mother might infer that the latter is caused by the former, when, in fact, Johnny did not eat his lima beans simply because he hates them. This fallacy is called *post hoc propter hoc*. One of my worries about The Toronto Blessing relates to this fallacy. Explanations about how manifestations lead to blessing can be given without proper attention to other factors at work in the person.
- **Make sure that conclusions follow from adequate evidence and support.** If I state that this book is infallible because I am left-handed, this would be viewed as absurd (even by most left-handed people). I would have to provide evidence to support the underlying assumption that left-handed people are infallible. In logic, this is called a *non sequitur*. Consider the argument that The Toronto Blessing is not of God because it causes division. The underlying premise here is that all division is wrong. That reasoning is faulty because critics of The Toronto Blessing also cause division, and, more importantly, Jesus himself caused division in his day. The real issue is whether there has to be division because some momentous issues of truth and goodness are at stake.
- **Do not accept clichés or popular sayings uncritically.** It is now common to hear Vineyard supporters say that "God reveals the heart by offending the mind." The point has some merit, but its anti-intellectual tone is troubling, especially since Jesus says to love God with "all your heart . . . *and* with all your mind" (Luke 10:27; italics added).
- **Do not "stack the deck."** On controversial items where one feels strongly, it is tempting to ignore evidence that goes against our pet theories. Those who call The Toronto Blessing demonic will focus on a few isolated incidents of extreme behavior and neglect the thousands of people who have been strengthened in Christian faith. Likewise, those who like to think of this renewal

as the Third Great Awakening ignore the reality that this renewal has not significantly impacted Canadian culture or even Toronto culture.

- **Be wary of generalization.** It is impossible to say everything with complete precision, and generalizations cannot be avoided. But while generalizations may be accurate, they can also be misleading. For example, it is generally true that the preaching at the Airport Vineyard could be better, but to say that Vineyard members or leaders do not care about the Bible is a gross over-statement.

- **Remember that the truth is not always in the middle.** The philosopher Aristotle taught that virtue lies between extremes. He did not, however, teach that *truth* was stationed similarly between two extremes. The truth may sometimes be a balance between two polar opposites, but not always. If one person says you have ten hands and another says two, does this mean you have six? Consider the view that The Toronto Blessing is massive delusion, bordering on the demonic. I do not believe this is true, but it is not false simply because it is an extreme position. I would suggest it is false for other reasons.

- **Do not take ideas or people out of context.** This is so easily done in heated debate. Consider, for example, John Arnott's statement that this renewal is not first about evangelism. Out of context, some critics could say that John does not care about soul-winning. But if you read his whole view, he is simply saying that the church must be renewed before it can become successful in evangelism.

Spiritual Discernment

Of course, fundamentally the discipline of testing the spirits involves spiritual discernment more than logical analysis. While knowing how to think plays an important role, the guidance of the Spirit is more crucial. What does spiritual discernment mean as we think about The Toronto Blessing and Holy Laughter?

One essential component in discernment is a readiness to admit weakness and limitation in that very gift. Since pride ruins everything, a humble recognition of one's limited understanding is a proper approach in testing the spirits. Mike Bickle took up my invitation to share with readers of this book his own learning in this area. He writes:

> I believe it is essential for all people involved in the subjective aspects of the Holy Spirit to be self-critical and teachable. To be defensive and resistant toward those who criticize us is to miss valuable opportunites to grow in wisdom. I realize it is more difficult to receive from people that do not favor our doctrinal position. However, most of us are not very good at being self-critical; thus, the Lord provides us with life-saving wisdom through others that we might not appreciate. This has happened to me on several occasions. It was at first offensive and even painful, but eventually it yields the peacable fruit of righteousness. The easiest path is to have a teachable heart that assumes that we have less than God's perfect wisdom and purity. We can thus expect to be adjusted by others on a regular basis.

Spiritual discernment also means a willingness to abandon shortcuts that lead nowhere in return for the more demanding disciplines of the spiritual life that produce eternal fruit. One thing that worries many observers of the charismatic world is its readiness to adopt a quick-fix approach to spirituality. Under the confident guise of being spiritual, gullibility and foolishness can reign as the charismatic masses follow one passing fad after another.

Lastly, spiritual discernment demands that we resist, as best we can, the penchant to judge the hearts of others. At this point, claims about being Spirit-filled or knowing the things of the Spirit are no guarantee of discernment. One has only to think of the sad cases involving Jim Bakker, Robert Tilton, Peter Poppoff, and Jimmy Swaggart to realize that we so easily misread the real situation in our own lives and the lives of others.

Three

John Wimber and
the Vineyard

In 1991 I was asked by Larry Matthews, the editor of *The Canadian Baptist*, to do an analysis of the Vineyard movement.[1] The magazine had earlier printed an ad for a Vineyard conference, which prompted a letter war over Baptists' support for the Vineyard movement.

I expected my assignment to be a rather simple task, since I thought that an analysis of a popular charismatic Christian group would pose no serious problems. I know better now, for a war had been waging over John Wimber and the Vineyard. The controversy over The Toronto Blessing has only added fuel to the fire.

However, one cannot understand The Toronto Blessing without some attention to the larger Vineyard movement and its famous leader. Serious allegations against Wimber's theology and credibility, which serve as a background to many of the suspicions about interpreting the renewal at the Airport Vineyard, must be examined.

Background to the Vineyard

John Wimber has become, over the last decade, a recognized leader in the Christian church. Being the center of attention has its drawbacks. When I visited Vineyard headquarters in the summer of 1991, Wimber's associates told me of his being unable to eat in a restaurant in southern California without someone approaching him for conversation or prayer. Fame has its blessings, yet there is also a price to pay. The attention and relentless criticism that accompanies it have made many in the Vineyard movement wary.

For example, one night in the fall of 1991 I phoned Wimber's son Sean. I was checking with him about a testimony I had heard that he had been helped through supernatural "words of knowledge" from prophets Bob Jones and Paul Cain. For a few moments Sean talked freely, and then our conversation was interrupted. Sean's wife became suspicious that I might be another person looking for "dirt" to discredit his father. Fortunately, I was able to convince Sean of my integrity, and we continued to talk. He confirmed the reports that I had heard about his renewal in faith.

A careful, scholarly account of the life of John Wimber must still be written, but the main events in his spiritual journey are recorded in many popular books and articles. Wimber has made it clear that he has no intention of writing an autobiography, though he has been open to interviews about his life and views.

Wimber was born in 1934 in the American Midwest. His alcoholic father left the family when John, an only child, was very young. He had no introduction to Christian faith in his youth. In 1955 he married his wife, Carol, a nominal Roman Catholic.

Gifted in music, he began his career as a writer for the rock group The Righteous Brothers. According to Wimber, the group was not composed of brothers nor were they righteous. His "worldly" success may have prepared him to handle fame and international attention when the Vineyard later became known around the world.

John and Carol separated in 1962, but their marriage was saved, so they believe, when John turned to God for help. His first experience in healing came when he prayed for his son Sean who had been severely stung by a horde of bees. John's report of this healing has been confirmed by Sean's older brother Tim, who discussed with me his clear memories of the event.

In the early 1970s John Wimber served as copastor of an evangelical Quaker Church in southern California. From 1974 to 1978 he worked with the Fuller Institute of Evangelism and Church

Growth. In 1977 Carol was working with a growing home prayer group, and the next year John became its pastor.

A year later John's healing ministry began, rooted in his memory of Sean's healing, his own gift in tongues when he was a young Christian, and his wife's rather dramatic experience of tongues in September, 1976. Both John and Carol had been strongly taught against glossolalia (the technical term for speaking in tongues), and it only reemerged in Wimber's life when Carol awoke speaking in tongues after dreaming about her objections to the practice.

After his Quaker days, Wimber became identified with Chuck Smith's group of Calvary Chapels. In 1982, Wimber left Calvary Chapel and became leader of a small group of churches known as the Vineyard, founded in 1974 by Kenn Gulliksen. Though Kenn had started the Vineyard movement, he relinquished the leadership reins to Wimber out of conviction that his gifts lay elsewhere and that Wimber would bring a visionary dynamic to the movement.

Several factors contributed to Wimber's international fame. On Mother's Day in 1981, Wimber's church experienced a revival among hundreds of young people. Wimber, shaken by some of the radical behavior in the service, stayed up late into the night, asking God for confirmation of its divine authenticity. Around 6:00 A.M. he got a call from a pastor friend in Colorado, Tom Stipe, who felt convicted by the Lord to call and offer Wimber encouragement. Tom, feeling foolish, expected Wimber to be asleep and irritated by the call. Stipe confirmed with me Wimber's account of this pivotal event.

In January, 1982, Wimber started teaching the course MC510 at Fuller Theological Seminary in Pasadena—a course entitled "Signs and Wonders and Church Growth." This class acquired worldwide interest after *Christian Life* magazine published a special report (October, 1982) on the Wimber-Fuller story. At about the same time, Wimber began a teaching ministry specifically designed to restore the gifts of the Spirit to the laity.

For the first two years things went well for Wimber. Then in February, 1984, his good friend David Watson, a leading renewal leader in England, died of cancer, a shock and a grievous loss to Wimber. Wimber had expected Watson to be cured of cancer. Blaine Cook, then a prominent Vineyard leader, said on BBC radio at the time: "Satan murdered David Watson."[2]

In 1985 Fuller Seminary put Wimber's course on hold. A significant doctrinal battle had developed over him, complaints were surfacing about his lack of academic training, and some among the faculty became jealous over his popularity. Students were signing up by the hundreds for the course, which included practical "clinics" where they participated in prayers for healing. Fuller later reinstated the course, and though the turmoil hurt Wimber deeply, he continued as an adjunct faculty member until 1992.[3]

In June, 1986, Wimber suffered a heart attack, but he recovered and continued his leadership of the Vineyard Church in Anaheim and of Vineyard Ministries International, the organization founded in 1982 to promote his teaching, healing, and music ministry. In 1995 he retired from both official appointments, though he clearly remains the Vineyard's international leader and ultimate voice of authority.

Analysis of the Vineyard would be relatively simple if it stopped at 1987, the year in which Wimber and some of his associates published a work called *Riding the Third Wave*, a balanced presentation of Vineyard ideology and practice. This book was advertised as "a thrilling, up-to-the-minute account of the Holy Spirit's work in our day."[4] However, in the following year, John Wimber told his followers that the Lord had revealed to him that the Vineyard was actually in desperate condition in 1987. He claims he repented, though without knowing specifically what sins were threatening the Vineyard's ministry.

Mike Bickle, an energetic and powerful preacher from Kansas City, offered Wimber encouragement and advice in late 1987 and early 1988. He went on to tell him about the supernatural ministry of Bob Jones and Paul Cain and other prophets connected with Bickle's Kansas City Fellowship. In the summer and fall of 1988 Wimber embraced the prophetic movement out of Kansas. In 1990

Mike Bickle's Kansas City Fellowship became known as Metro Vineyard, under the umbrella of the Association of Vineyard Churches.

The issue of the Vineyard and the Kansas City prophets is significant and complex and will be dealt with in a later chapter. However, it seems odd that in 1987 Wimber and his colleagues had offered the Christian world "a thrilling, up-to-the-minute account" of the Spirit's work, while the very next year Wimber said the Spirit told him the Vineyard was in bad shape. There are ways, I suppose, that this dichotomy can be harmonized. But this is an example of a serious weakness in the charismatic and Pentecostal tradition. The Holy Spirit is invoked with too much ease and regularity, leading to contradiction in claims and confusion among those who listen carefully to their leaders.

This concern is only one among the legion of allegations and criticisms that have been made against Wimber. We will now consider some of these charges.

Criticisms Against Wimber's Theology

When I began my study of the Vineyard in 1991, I was amazed by the number of charges raised against John Wimber. Some of these had to do with misgivings about the prophetic element, but most constituted complaints about the original Vineyard vision, including complaints directed against Wimber's personal integrity and beliefs.

In a recent publication Wayne Grudem lists thirty-eight accusations that have circulated against Wimber and the Vineyard.[5] The list could be much longer since Grudem restricted himself to those charges raised in the book *Power Religion* and in John Armstrong's critique in *The Standard* (October 1990-July 1991), the monthly publication of the Baptist General Conference.[6]

Many of the stronger objections to Wimber are bizarre and outlandish, such as: (1) Wimber is a New Ager; (2) Wimber does not believe the Bible; (3) Wimber wants to follow the Pope; (4) Wimber does not care about the Cross; (5) Wimber is an anti-intellectual zealot; (6) Wimber does not preach the gospel; (7) Wimber gets his power from Satan; (8) Wimber is working towards the One World Church; (9) Wimber does not believe in Jesus; and (10) Wimber does not care about heresy.

In my 1992 article in *The Canadian Baptist* I listed some of these complaints and wrote that "such charges are simply false." In my naiveté, I thought such foolish allegations would be recognized as such. However, a pastor from British Columbia complained about my giving "no references to support" my argument on Wimber's behalf.[7]

Consider, then, the allegation that Wimber is a New Ager. Let me give several reasons why I think the accusation is absurd. (1) The doctrinal statement of the Vineyard is thoroughly biblical.[8] (2) Wimber's books contain no positive references to New Age writers. (3) His preaching is focused on Christ as the only Savior and Lord. (4) In interviews Wimber's views bear no relationship to New Age thinking. (5) One entire issue of *Equipping the Saints* (the Vineyard's magazine) dealt with "Confronting the New Age."[9]

Other questions raised about the Vineyard involve balance and emphasis in Christian teaching and life. For example, some have charged Wimber with neglecting the role of suffering in sanctification—a possible inference from Vineyard emphasis on healing. However, Wimber has published teaching on the nature and utility of suffering,[10] and he is open about his own emotional and physical pain.

Other Christians question Wimber's emphasis on healing in relation to what is called the Health and Wealth Gospel. Wimber has never said that all sickness is the result of a lack of faith, nor has he given allegiance to the teachings of the Word Faith movement, which imply that faithful Christians will never be sick. When Larry Matthews and I interviewed Wimber in the fall of 1991, we asked him specifically about the role of medicine and faith. He replied by showing us some medication he takes regularly for his heart condition. Tragically, there are those in the Word Faith tradition who have not followed Wimber's balance. Under the guise of "faith," certain healers have brought serious sickness and even death to gullible followers.

We turn to several general points about the Vineyard movement. First, the rhetoric about the miraculous is not matched on the whole by the reality of such miracles in the Vineyard's history, though this is not to deny the reality of some miracle stories. But given the weight that Wimber has placed on "signs and wonders," one would expect the movement to be flooded with medical reports and with detailed, careful testimonies of miraculous healings.

After recounting several miracles stories from Wimber, John MacArthur writes that he finds them "utterly preposterous."[11] There are, however, only two things that give a Christian the right to deliver such a verdict: (1) if the miracle is done in the name and power of a false god (in which case the miracle is leading someone to idolatry), and (2) if a specific story turns out to be false. In principle, then, I disagree with MacArthur, for he did not take the time to confirm or disconfirm the various reports. However, he does make a larger point that Vineyard leaders should note. Miracle reports must be confirmed from their end; the burden of proof is on them. The one major investigation by David Lewis is not enough for an area where there is so much hype.[12]

The Vineyard movement also needs to be far more cautious about its elitism. Wimber has said that he cares deeply about other Christian groups. According to him, "Highest priority . . . is for peace and unity in the body of Christ."[13] We can accept this at face value, but there is an unconscious superiority complex at work in the movement, manifested in several ways. (1) In its constant talk about not being a denomination, the Vineyard manifests a certain elitism—similar to Christians who brag that they are not part of a "religion." (2) The emphasis on signs and wonders automatically produces, in many Vineyard followers, an elite feeling. (3) Vineyard has picked up the unspiritual view that the charismatic world has a corner on the Spirit.

Regarding the "unconscious superiority complex" referred to above, this relates to the rivers that run deep in a movement, ones that are often hard to recognize. Vineyard members do not get up at meetings and say, "Hello, we are the only show in town." Like most Christian groups, their pride is masked. In reality, most religious groups (Christian and otherwise) have an underlying elitism. Our respective traditions usually teach us to be snobs, though we learn how to brag while sounding holy. In my own teaching at a transdenominational seminary I have often heard students admit to being surprised that other denominations might be Christian.[14]

The Briefing Report

The April 24, 1990, issue of *The Briefing*, an Australian Anglican magazine from St. Matthias Anglican Church in Sydney, has done more damage to the Vineyard's reputation than perhaps any other single source. In March, 1990, leaders from that church interviewed John Wimber, Paul Cain, and Jack Deere, who were in Sydney for a Vineyard conference. Copies of the original report, entitled "John Wimber: Friend or Foe?" circulated widely and were reprinted as a separate booklet. The accusations raised by this magazine have been passed on as standard criticisms of John Wimber and the Vineyard, accusing the Vineyard of essentially being a cult.

Unfortunately, Vineyard leaders, following John Wimber's long-standing policy of not responding to criticism, took too long to reply to the accusations. Wimber had decided early in his ministry to avoid public disputes with fellow Christians, continuing in his ministry in spite of false accusations. He was following a guideline that was in keeping with the example of Nehemiah: "Do a great work for God and leave your critics at the gate" (cf. Neh. 6:3).

Of course, even good guidelines have their limits. The Australian critics were credible Christian leaders, and it sounded as if they had done their research. The most notorious charges were that Wimber did not make the Cross central in his theology and that Jack Deere (formerly of Dallas Theological Seminary) denied the sufficiency of the Bible. Graham Banister also wrote an article saying that Deere admitted that he did not know what the gospel was. Wimber should have responded sooner, but it was not until May, 1992, that Deere published a thirty-one page reply.[15]

I have read both *The Briefing* report and Jack Deere's detailed reply. If Christians are forced to decide this polarized question on the basis of these two documents, the evidence decidedly favors John Wimber as a friend of the Christian church. Deere's sustained response is, in my opinion, a death blow to the Australian critique. He may not be right on every point, but he clearly shows the bias and carelessness that went on in the grilling of Wimber, Cain, and himself. How anyone can read John Wimber's books or hear his personal testimony and think that our salvation rests in anything other than the Cross is difficult to imagine.

As to Deere's denial of the sufficiency of Scripture, his reply makes plain the only way in which he would deny this classic doctrine. If someone suggests that the Bible alone is all that we need, he would say that we need Jesus too! This is no more heretical than pointing out that we sometimes use other books besides the Bible to help us in our Christian lives.

Did Jack Deere admit to not knowing the gospel? Before answering that question, surely his track record of study and teaching should force us to give him the benefit of the doubt. After all, years of work at Dallas Seminary should at least indicate that he understands and accepts the basics of the gospel. In point of fact, Jack Deere does understand the essence of the gospel, as his reply makes plain.

Deeper Levels of Discernment

There is one larger danger about the Vineyard movement, however, that does need sober examination. Earlier I spoke about the danger of hasty assessments of the Spirit that break down under a more reflective probing. In 1987 we were offered a "thrilling, up-to-the-minute" ride on the Third Wave, while the next year the Holy Spirit apparently told Wimber that the movement had been in desperate shape. As a result, from 1988 through 1991 Wimber embraced the prophetic movement out of Kansas City. The reports from Vineyard conferences hailed this new move of God, and the Holy Spirit seemed to be back in full force.

Vineyard insiders realize that Wimber has now moved beyond the prophetic movement, though not by repudiating this gift in total. The prophetic glory days, allegedly flowing out of the Spirit, are over. We will examine the Kansas City prophets saga in a later chapter. For now what needs scrutiny is the Vineyard's turbulent ride on the Third Wave. For a movement so confident of its obedience to the Spirit, the ups and downs of the last decade suggest that there must be more caution in making dramatic claims about the Spirit's work. Is the fault because there is such pressure to be on a continual high? Is there insufficient attention being paid to the valleys of Christian experience?

The Vineyard movement may be self-absorbed because it is a young movement and because it has attracted so much attention. Todd Hunter, National Coordinator of the Vineyard Churches, said recently that the media attention is out of proportion to the small numbers of Vineyard followers and churches. Has the quest for signs and wonders fed into a more subtle desire for fame and glory?

This question may seem antagonistic. But I am asking it to invite Vineyard leaders and followers to realize the need for prolonged and subtle analysis, for a probing and deeper level of Spirit discernment. While it is true that too much can be made of self-analysis, it will not hurt the Vineyard to be more reflective and careful about its self-assessment of life in obedience to the Spirit.

Conclusion

Analysis and response to The Toronto Blessing can be short-circuited by a premature response to John Wimber and the Vineyard. A negative bias has predisposed some to dismiss the recent phenomenon as simply more evidence that the Vineyard is a cult, or at least a dangerous sub-Christian group.

This chapter makes plain that there is no solid evidence to dismiss Wimber or the Vineyard in this manner. Whatever weaknesses exist in his theology, he does not deserve to be treated as a heretic.

Likewise, Vineyard churches subscribe to an evangelical doctrinal statement, and their pastors see themselves in communion with all followers of evangelical Christianity.

These positive comments do not obligate one, however, to view Wimber as infallible or the movement he leads as beyond reproof. Far more than many other famous Christian leaders, Wimber is willing to admit mistakes and errors. Thus, he will not mind that examination of The Toronto Blessing be done with rigorous attention to the full counsel of Scripture. The movement's own history suggests that it is prone to some confusion about its central aims and identity. A call to discernment is in order and should not unduly worry a movement that believes that the Holy Spirit offers such a powerful gift to the church.

Four

The Holy Ghost Bartender

On Saturday, March 18, 1995, I flew to New York City in order to attend a worship service in Long Island the next day. Rodney Howard-Browne was starting a six-day crusade with Pastor Tony D'Onofrio at Upper Room Ministries, a large church in Dix Hills, about forty-five minutes from Manhattan. I felt it was crucial to hear Howard-Browne for myself.

Rodney Howard-Browne's name is synonymous with Holy Laughter. A native of South Africa, Howard-Browne has been holding revival campaigns in the United States since 1987. In the last three years he has become one of the leading voices in the charismatic world.[1] His meetings at the Carpenter's Home Church in Lakeland, Florida, and at Oral Roberts University have reached legendary status in the charismatic and Pentecostal world.

I had read so many conflicting reports about Howard-Browne that I was hoping my two days in Long Island would provide an adequate basis to help sort through the polarized reactions to his teaching and ministry. A number of significant attacks on him and his credibility had already appeared. In fact, some people completely dismiss The Toronto Blessing by linking it with Rodney Howard-Browne.

While in Long Island, I attended three Sunday worship services and one Monday morning teaching session. I had an opportunity to talk with Rodney Howard-Browne for about a half hour on Sunday afternoon. He agreed to do a formal interview the next afternoon.

Common Misconceptions

My trip to New York did not settle every issue about Holy Laughter, but some popular criticisms about Rodney Howard-Browne were laid to rest. Most important, it is simply not true that he does not care about teaching the Bible. In all four meetings he taught at length from Scripture, and in the interview it was obvious that he had a ready grasp of biblical teaching. I have examined some of his many videotapes and read his two books. Scriptural exposition and teaching are prominent both in his video series and in his printed material.

There is no doubt that some of his videos consist mainly of personal testimonies and clips of people overcome with the "anointing" of the Holy Spirit. One might legitimately desire him to be more focused in his preaching or to seek better and clearer exegesis. However, none of this amounts to saying that he does not care about the Bible.

It is also misleading to say that Howard-Browne "manipulates" his congregations into Holy Laughter. I saw little in Long Island that would warrant such an allegation, although this does not mean he is simply a bystander or is totally passive in leading worship. Granted, there are occasions where his videotapes show him instructing someone about how to be open to Holy Laughter, but this is not pervasive in his revival meetings.

The picture of Rodney Howard-Browne as some sort of stage magician who knows how to work the charismatic crowds into frenzied Holy Laughter is misleading. This is especially true if one suggests *conscious* intent on his part to deceive and grossly manipulate the congregation. After examining his videos, listening to him in his meetings in Long Island, and spending several hours in conversation, I do not believe his ministry is built on such a dubious foundation.

In his audiotape on "The Counterfeit Revival," Hank Hanegraaff has argued that Howard-Browne engages in overt manipulation of the audience. I agree with Hank on many issues and have deep admiration for his work as president of Christian Research Institute. On this particular point, however, I think his criticism is unfair, especially if he is implying that Howard-Browne is cold and calculated in his control of the congregation.

Of course, psychological forces are at work in charismatic worship, as they are in any act of worship. We are psychological creatures. Obviously, Rodney's style and energy impact the audience, sometimes in a powerful way. However, Hanegraaff's suggestion that Rodney uses embedded commands and other control tactics on the congregation is, in my view, too severe.

My main reasons for disagreement with Hanegraaff are twofold. (1) My personal impression of Howard-Browne is not as negative as his. I should note that Hank and a close friend were actually singled out by Howard-Browne at a revival meeting in Melodyland in January, 1995. Rodney was upset at Hank and the friend for talking back and forth during the worship service, and he approached them to be quiet or leave. Howard-Browne also implied that Hank and other critics might be in danger of blasphemy against the Holy Spirit for their prohibition against what God is doing.

(2) As to my specific disagreement with Hanegraaff's views about manipulation, charismatic crowds need no master manipulator in order to be ready for displays of emotional and religious ecstasy. In Long Island, the congregation was bursting with energy and anticipation even before the start of the service. The style of worship was typical of modern Pentecostalism: powerful music, enthusiastic congregational participation, and plenty of strong emotion. In this context, Rodney Howard-Browne's style and leadership seemed rather restrained.

Claims Beyond Holy Laughter

One evening in a phone conversation with Rodney Howard-Browne, I raised an issue with him that has a significant bearing on the integrity of his entire ministry. In his books and videos he makes stupendous claims about miraculous events in his own life that go far beyond the issue of Holy Laughter. Rodney admitted that if he is not telling the truth about these astounding items, then his role as "the bartender of the new wine" is seriously undermined.

Note that I am not referring to his retelling of miraculous events in the lives of other people. For example, Howard-Browne tells the story of Smith Wigglesworth, who has reportedly brought a relative back from the dead at a funeral. Howard-Browne states: "When the gift of faith comes on you, you don't take no for an answer! [Wigglesworth] bent down, picked the corpse up again, slammed it against the wall, and thundered, 'I told you to walk!' And the man walked!"

No, it is Howard-Browne's own personal claims of miracles that are at issue. They force one, as he himself acknowledges, to choose one of three options: He is a liar, he is deluded, or he is telling the truth.

In his work *The Touch of God*, he talks about healing a woman who was on her deathbed with cancer. After he prayed for her, she recovered and went shopping the next day.[2] He also tells the story of his mother being healed from severe breaks to her left arm. In my interview with him, he said that he saw this himself as a young boy and that it made a lasting impression on him and his whole family. He offered to have his mother call me so that I could hear directly from her about this event.

There are other accounts of God's miraculous touch in his life story. In *Flowing in the Holy Ghost* Howard-Browne gives this case about the word of the Lord:

> I was in a meeting in Tennessee, minding my own business, when the voice of the Lord came to me and said, "That lady over there—call her out right now." She was standing by herself.
>
> He said, "I'm going to give her a miracle: the thing that she's desired."
>
> As I began to prophecy, I knew she was going to have a baby, but she was standing by herself—and when I looked at her hands, she wasn't wearing a ring!
>
> I thought, "O God, I have blown it!"

But I said to the woman, "Sister, that which you have desired, and that which is impossible in the natural, shall come to pass. God will give you a miracle. You've been desiring to have ... a ... a *baby!*" Eventually I said it. I thought to myself, "Look, I'm so deep now, I might as well jump in all the way."

She burst out crying. She was married; she just hadn't put her rings on that day. And she and her husband desperately wanted to have a child.

A year later I went back to their church and I held that baby in my arms. It came to pass, as God said.[3]

Rodney Howard-Browne told me that he would have no problem with providing me details for these claims at a later time. What is important to note at the outset is the supernatural claim he makes and the way that such stupendous accounts allow limited options in interpretation.

Interview with Rodney Howard-Browne

In a spacious sitting area at Upper Room Ministries, I had an extensive interview with Rodney Howard-Browne. We were with one of his assistants and several of the staff from the Dix Hills church, including the Senior Pastor Tony D'Onofrio. My brother Bob Beverley was with me for the interview. He is a Baptist pastor and psychotherapist and had traveled to Long Island from his home in Hyde Park, New York, in order to join me for the Sunday evening and Monday meetings.

The following is an edited version of the interview. I have simplified my questions for the sake of clarity and edited his responses to give the heart of his views, though all the words used from Howard-Browne are taken verbatim from the tape. Some of our conversation was "off the record," but, overall, he was candid and clear in his response to queries and criticisms.

JB: What is your connection with the Word Faith movement?

RHB: "I think what people been trying to do for a long time is try to polarize me, because if they can do that, then they put me into a camp. I don't consider myself part of a camp."

JB: How would you describe yourself then?

RHB: "I would say I'm more old time Pentecostal. [But] I can't be polarized into a camp, and I think that's what people are trying to do, 'cause then they can write me off. And basically, it's the same thing with the Holy Laughter."

JB: What about the report in the *Christian Research Journal* that denies your claim to have been an assistant pastor at the Rhema Church in South Africa?

RHB: "What, did they get a quote from them? Well, I have a business card that says I was."

JB: Is there anything that you've said or done publicly that you really regret?

RHB: "I can't think of anything, I mean if you brought something up and I thought about it, then maybe I'd say, 'Well, I guess I shouldn't have said that.' Let me say this to you. I'm totally established in what I believe. I'm not confused in what I believe, I'm not saying that we can't grow and learn, because we're growing and learning all the time, but as far as basic doctrine is concerned, I'm convinced that I know. I feel I'm on a rock as far as basic doctrine and stuff like that."

JB: Do you know much about The Toronto Blessing?

RHB: "All I know is that a guy by the name of Randy Clark came to the meeting, and God fell on him and he came forward. I remember him coming to me with his hands ablaze and said, 'My hands are burning.' I said, 'Yeah, that's the anointing. You know what it's for?' I said, 'Go back to your church and lay hands on everything that moves.' And he went back to his church, laid hands on everything that moved, the next week he went to Toronto and the rest is history."

JB: Are there elements of The Toronto Blessing where you have disagreements?

RHB: "Well, first of all, we don't have any barking or roaring in our meetings. If you bark like a dog, we'll give you dog food. If you roar like a lion, we'll put you in the zoo. If you cluck like a chicken, we'll give you bird seed. Now, I made that statement because I just wanted people to know that there was some order in the service."

JB: What about lion roaring as a prophetic sign?

RHB: "Alright, I know that another friend of mine was ministering, and a man came up to him in the meeting on all fours and was roaring like a lion and said, 'I'm the lion in the tribe of Judah.' And my friend looked at him and said, 'I'm the lion tamer, and sit down and shut up.' But again, I don't want to get into [a debate with] the Toronto people because I'm happy with what's happening in Toronto."

JB: Was there anything in last night's meeting that bothered you?

RHB: "Maybe there were one or two people reacting in the flesh."

JB: But would you admit that it is sometimes just people doing their thing?

RHB: "Well, I don't know. I mean I don't want to say yes, because I don't know. It could be, but we don't know. How do we know? So you can only really know when God shows you. You can't go by any physical jerks or manifestations or whatever other than the fruit in the person's life afterwards or talking to them and saying, 'What did God do to you, what happened?' If I'm in a meeting and somebody is doing something and I start getting grieved down here, I stop it. If it doesn't grieve me, if I don't feel grieved or feel uncomfortable here, I don't stop it. Do you understand what I'm saying? I've got grieved by people sitting with their arms folded, critical."

JB: Why do you preach and allow your preaching to be drowned out by Holy Laughter?

RHB: "Because there are some people that aren't laughing and there's some people that are sitting and really receiving, and so the whole thing is [a case like in] Acts 10:44 [where it says that] while Peter spoke these words, the Holy Ghost fell."

JB: What would you do in a case where one person is sharing a deep personal story in a congregation, and then his painful sharing is drowned out by someone doing Holy Laughter?

RHB: "Let me say this: In my meeting if one person was doing that [hurting the person sharing], I'd stop it [the laughter]. But when it's happening to thousands of people, it's different."

JB: Would you continue to preach if the laughter was so loud no one could hear you?

RHB: "Sometimes the anointing of God is on me, and I'm totally oblivious to what's happening out there. I'm totally lost. I've been in meetings and been totally lost. I'm under the presence of God and busy ministering. I can get the tape later and listen to it, 'cause it's all coming live onto the tape and it'll be above the noise and whatever."

JB: What do you think of the reservations that Stephen Strang expressed about you in the *Charisma* issue?

RHB: "I met with Steve Thursday and Friday, and Steve is behind us, his wife's been totally touched, his son's been touched. Stephen's a journalist, so he's got to say that [to have balance]. [But] I believe this very strongly, that there is a dividing line coming between those who want to move with the things of God and those who don't want to move with the things of God."

JB: Do you see how a lot of your comments could be construed as anti-intellectual?

RHB: "When you're dealing with the Spirit of God, you're dealing with reasoning and man on the one side."

JB: Let me be more precise. Are you opposed to Christians who want to be teachers and professors, who want to use their godly wisdom and intellect to study doctrine?

RHB: "Not at all."

JB: But are you not complaining about people using their fleshly reason?

RHB: "To try and explain God. They'll make a comment like this, 'Well, this can't be God.' Then I come back to them and say, 'OK fine, if this is not God, you mean to tell me everything you've seen is God? Or you've seen everything God's ever going to do?'"

JB: One of your statements from your booklet *The Coming Revival* has been used to say that you do not care if the devil and the flesh become manifest in a church service.

RHB: "I mean I want something to happen. I want God to touch people, but I don't just want the devil moving in the service."

JB: Why don't you just say this: "I don't want the flesh or the devil in any service"?

RHB: "I don't want him. But the thing is, we end up with them [the flesh and the devil], because he is in with people. I mean you can say that, 'I don't want the flesh and the devil.'"

JB: Why have you praised William Branham?

RHB: "William Branham went off in the last part of his life. He was originally a man of God. My dad was delivered from smoking cigarettes, sixty per day and a pipe, sitting in one of William's services in Africa, many years ago."

JB: You claim in one of your books that God might transport people. What are you saying there?

RHB: "Well, just like in the book of Acts—just like Philip."

JB: Do you believe in miracle cloths?

RHB: "I believe in Acts 19:11–12: 'God did extraordinary miracles through Paul, so that even handkerchiefs and aprons that had touched him were taken to the sick, and their illnesses were cured and the evil spirits left them.'"

JB: Do you believe in evangelists sending out mass-produced hankies?

RHB: "No. [But] people come ask me for my handkerchief all the time, and I pray over it and let them take it home."

JB: Have you heard any amazing reports back?

RHB: "This happened in Africa several years ago. [A lady] came to me, and she said, 'I don't know what to do, I really got to do something about my husband.' So we prayed over this cloth. So she went home; she cut the thing in half, sewed one in his pyjamas in the jacket, the other half in his pillow. And every morning for about three weeks she'd come home, the pillow was lying on the side of the room, and he'd take off his jacket in the night. And then about three weeks later God totally saved him and set him free. So I really believe the power of God was in the cloth that went into him and set him free. But man can make an idol out of anything."

JB: Would you comment on your mother's healing?

RHB: "I was there when she cut the cast off. The arm broke in three places. It was such a bad break. The doctor told us, 'This is a terrible break.' She slipped in the mud and fell, put the cast on. She was sitting at home, Saturday afternoon. I know the next day she cut it off—four days in total that the cast was on. And they had a reel to reel tape (this is 1960, whatever). I was about five—she would probably know the dates; I'm not really one for dates. But they were listening to this tape, and the power of God fell on her, and her hand started tingling, burning like fire. And our pastor was there. He walked up and laid hands on her, and she knew she'd been healed. [She went into the bathroom and] filled the tub. She took a razor blade and cut the cast off—it was plaster of paris. And I'm standing outside the door, crying, 'Mom, don't do it, 'cause your arm's going to fall off.' She was totally healed by the power of God. She drove the car [to see the doctor]. Now the motor car in South Africa is on the other side; she has to change with this hand [of her broken arm]. She changed the gears, drove to the doctor; they took about thirty or forty X rays and just couldn't believe it."

JB: Is that doctor still alive?

RHB: "I don't know. He could be. But the whole thing is this: What do we have to do now in our lives to get proof for everything that happens to us? But the evidence is, her arm was broken and it got healed. I saw it, she saw it, my father saw it, the rest of the family saw it. I mean, what else constitutes evidence? Here's my thing: I don't have the time to run around to answer all the critics. I'm too busy preaching the gospel."

JB: In your book *The Touch of God*, you say, "Nothing Jesus did was because he was the Son of God." Are you denying the deity of Christ while he was on earth?

RHB: "He laid aside his royal robes of deity in the sense he had to take on human flesh."

JB: So, you don't mean in your book that he wasn't the Son of God?

RHB: "He was all God and all man. Acts 10:38 also says how God anointed Jesus with the Holy Ghost. There's the Godhead, the Trinity. Well, have they used that [quote] against me?"

JB: Yes, the quotation has been used to say that you deny that Jesus operated as the Son of God, that he only worked as a man.

RHB: "He was the God-Man."

JB: When you say nothing Jesus did was because he was the Son of God, were you simply intending to mean that he was human from birth and that his miracles were out of both humanity and divinity?

RHB: "Yes."

JB: How do you travel the world, how do you do what you are doing, and how do you maintain a family?

RHB: "We take our family with us. They are with me all the time. We home-school them on the road."

JB: Do you feel free to comment about money?

RHB: "I am blessed. I get a salary. My salary is set by the board."

JB: Are you free to say what that is?

RHB: "No, not right now. If we took five thousand ministries across America and had them all disclose their salaries, that's fine, I'll do it. Why would [my critics] want to bring the finances into it? They must be just looking for another thing to try to nail me on."

JB: What have you wrestled with through the years?

RHB: "I have a hard time believing that people can't believe that God is as awesome as he is. I really have a problem. I have a hard time dealing with Pharisees. I've always clashed with people that always wanted to argue about the power of God or the reality of God. I always seem to bump into them."

JB: Do you have trouble with the lack of discernment among Pentecostals or charismatics who fall for fake evangelists and healers?

RHB: "Here's the other side of it. You know God always honors people's faith. We had a guy in South Africa that was running around charging people for healings, and the thing is the people were getting healed because their faith was in God. But the guy died at fifty with cancer. So the whole thing is, the gospel is being preached, just like when the disciples came to Jesus and said there are other people down the road who have been using your name. He said, 'Leave them. If they're not against us, they are for us.' So that is the way I look at it."

JB: Does it bother you to be quoted as saying that it is often the Pentecostal churches that are dead?

RHB: "No. It is hard to have revival when you think you are revived."

JB: The Bible is really profound on the way we deceive ourselves.

RHB: "That's the whole thing. I just want to say this too: We don't only emphasize the power, we emphasize godly character. Our messages are repentance, consecration, godly character."

JB: There are accusations that you do not care about repentance.

RHB: "I just think that the time has come when we have to ignore the critics totally because they are getting totally ridiculous."

JB: Don't you think you should distinguish between those who want to obey the Bible and "test the Spirits" in the right way, and those who really are mean-spirited in their attacks?

RHB: "That's fine."

Bob Beverley: I've heard the dean of Harvard Divinity School twelve years ago. He said: "Remember the sin that preachers break most isn't adultery. It's 'Thou shalt not bear false witness against thy neighbor.'" I have never forgotten that.

RHB: "That's what Peter Jennings said to me: 'How come there is so much jealousy in the body of Christ?'"

The Word Faith Issue

Rodney Howard-Browne's connection with the Word Faith movement is sometimes noted in the critique of The Toronto Blessing. For example, Alan Morrison traces Howard-Browne's roots from the South African Rhema Church to Kenneth Hagin, the most influential Word Faith teacher in America, and then back to E. W.

Kenyon, who was influenced by the occult traditions of New Thought. Morrison states: "Surely the earthly ancestry of the 'Toronto Blessing'—regardless of any alleged benefits—provides a certain point to its dark spiritual origins."[4] Dave Roberts, on the other hand, defends Howard-Browne by saying that "heresy hunters delight in playing the guilt-by-association game."[5] This *ad hominem* jab will not suffice. What matters is whether or not the Word Faith tradition is so erroneous that Howard-Browne's contact and ministry with their leaders deserves serious criticism.

In 1993 Hank Hanegraaff released his powerful critique of the Word Faith movement under the title *Christianity in Crisis*. That book presents his concerns along five lines. (1) The movement has a faulty view of faith; (2) the leaders teach erroneous views about the deification of Christians; (3) Word Faith teachers misunderstand the atonement; (4) Word Faith teaching amounts to a materialistic worldview; and (5) the Word Faith leaders present a dangerous view of sickness and suffering.[6] Hanegraaff's style may not appeal to some readers, but the clarity of his message and his extensive documentation more than compensate for any quibbles over language or occasional lapses in logic. While I think his remark that "the Faith movement is every bit as cultic as the teachings of the Mormons, the Jehovah's Witnesses, and Christian Science"[7] is accurate only if understood as hyperbole, this work has served as a wake-up call about the overt heresies in the Word Faith tradition.

Consider, for example, this alleged prophecy from Jesus via Kenneth Copeland.

> Don't be disturbed when people accuse you of thinking you're God. Don't be disturbed when people accuse you of a fanatical way of life. Don't be disturbed when people put you down and speak harshly and roughly of you. They spoke that way of Me, should they not speak that way of you?
>
> The more you get to be like Me, the more they're going to think that way of you. They crucified Me for claiming that I was God. *But I didn't claim I was God*; I just claimed I walked with Him and that He was in Me. Hallelujah. That's what you're doing.

It is this kind of theology that is exposed by Hanegraaff.

Tragically, Word Faith teachers in general have chosen to ignore the message and simply attack the messenger. With the exception of Benny Hinn, they have shown no willingness to learn from criticism and repent for false and misleading teachings. The Christian church at large must maintain severe reserve about the writings of Word Faith teachers like Kenneth Hagin, Kenneth Copeland, and Frederick K. C. Price.

It is depressing to witness how powerful charismatic publishers and television empires have resorted to half-baked arguments, name-calling, and even divine threats against Hanegraaff in their rush to defend those in the Word Faith camp. It would have been far more noble for them simply to admit the dubious and bizarre side of Word Faith. Writing in 1993, Stephen Strang, the publisher of *Charisma*, used an editorial to dismiss Hank as a "stone thrower."[8] In the May, 1995 issue of this magazine, Lee Grady wrote a one-sided attack on Hanegraaff under the title, "Does the Church Need Heresy Hunters?" Grady has some legitimate concerns, but his article is marred by lack of balance and overstatement. Neither Strang or Grady give Hanegraaff enough credit for his courage in exposing the dubious and heretical elements in the Word Faith tradition.

William DeArteaga has defended the Word Faith tradition in his new work, *Quenching the Spirit*. His arguments seem desperate. For example, he tries valiantly to combat the evidence from D. R. McConnell's work, *A Different Gospel*, that Hagin plagiarized much of his writing from the books of E. W. Kenyon.[9] While DeArteaga admits that McConnell showed "that many of Hagin's books and pamphlets mirror earlier Kenyon texts word for word or sentence for sentence,"[10] he cannot live with the obvious implication of this reality. DeArteaga mentions Hagin's own defense that perhaps God gave him and Kenyon the same revelation word for word, but DeArteaga rejects this suggestion by stating that God would not embarrass Hagin in this fashion. He goes on to contend that "Hagin is a person of unquestioned integrity" and that this whole issue amounts to "unintentional plagiarism," rooted in Hagin's "almost perfect photographic memory."

There are several weaknesses in DeArteaga's defense. (1) Since DeArteaga disputes Hagin's own suggestion that the Lord is behind both texts, one must ask what "unquestioned integrity" Hagin has in his persistent claim that the Spirit gave the same words to both writers.[11] (2) The use of Hagin's alleged memory skills is strained. If Hagin could see pages from eight different Kenyon texts in his mind, would one not expect that his brain could also see eight different title pages or book covers? (3) As DeArteaga knows, Kenneth Hagin has allegedly been to heaven on numerous occasions. Is it too much to expect that Jesus would have taken the time to help Hagin with the serious issue of plagiarism? Hagin claims, like any famous Word Faith preacher, to have the ability to see into the demonic realm. The fact that he cannot see plagiarism in his own writings brings to mind C. S. Lewis's remark about those who claim to see fern-seed but cannot see elephants in broad daylight.[12]

This one case serves as an example of the kind of sloppy logic that pervades the defense of the Word Faith preachers. It also shows how people like DeArteaga adopt an unbiblical standard toward the great spiritual "giants" in that tradition. He holds them less accountable than the "average" person, whereas the Bible demands a higher standard of those who lead the church. Students at Rhema training schools would be disciplined for plagiarism, while Hagin, the founder, is excused.

Though I do not believe that Howard-Browne shares many of the extreme views of the Word Faith preachers, it would certainly help the cause of Christ if he were to use his enormous status in the Word Faith world to speak, even privately, a powerful prophetic word against the abuses in that tradition. If he does not do so, the divine threats against Hank Hanegraaff sound hollow indeed.

Associate Pastor at Rhema Bible Church?

After I returned to Toronto, I contacted Howard-Browne again to ask for verification of his claim that he was an associate pastor at the Rhema Bible Church in Johannesburg, South Africa. Writing in the *Christian Research Journal* (Winter, 1995), Perucci Ferraiuolo cited Gordon Kelmeyer, an administrative staff member at that church, to the effect that Howard-Browne was not an associate pastor there.

Howard-Browne responded to this allegation by saying that he had left Rhema before Kelmeyer came on staff. He claimed Kelmeyer was simply wrong. At Howard-Browne's request, Norman Robertson called me to confirm Rodney's claim. He had been on staff when Howard-Browne was hired, and he told me that Kelmeyer was, in fact, mistaken. I faxed a letter requesting a verdict from Peter Riggall, the top administrator of the Rhema Bible Church. He replied on April 12, 1995, with a letter that not only stated that Howard-Browne had pastoral status there, but he also sent a copy of an old business card, which indicated that Howard-Browne was an assistant pastor.

When I shared this update with Hank Hanegraaff, he stated that he would check into this report and would publicly retract any false information that had been given against Rodney Howard-Browne. The evidence so far suggests that Howard-Browne's view has been largely justified.

Concerns About Holy Laughter Revival?

On the bottom line, some concerns remain from my interaction with Rodney Howard-Browne and my experience of renewal meetings under his leadership. While I cannot find myself in sympathy with those severe critics who contend, for example, that Howard-Browne is imitating voodoo worship, caution is in order by way of helpful criticism.

(1) I think Howard-Browne needs to be more aware of the power of what can be called "crowd theology." The charismatic and Pentecostal traditions have always gone for the "big meeting," and the focus has been on the "man of God" who is able to overwhelm the crowds by his marvelous works. In the process, that crowd adulation simultaneously sweeps the healer or evangelist along in a

dance to some form of destruction, whether spiritual, financial, or moral.

In this regard, Howard-Browne should pay close attention to the work of David Harrell, Jr., as this leading historian has chronicled the successes and the misfortunes of leading Pentecostal revivalists of our century. In his two famous works, *All Things Are Possible* and *Oral Roberts: An American Life*, Harrell shows how easily the giants of the Pentecostal tradition have found it so hard to resist the pressures that come with the blessing of the masses.

(2) I believe that Rodney Howard-Browne should be aware of the anti-intellectual trends in his thought. These become especially disconcerting when they are matched with the underlying lack of intellectual rigor in the charismatic crowd. This combination leaves little room for self-criticism and self-awareness.

(3) Finally, I remain concerned that all the emphasis on Holy Laughter and other Spirit manifestations represents something that is out of focus in the light of Scripture. Granted, the Bible speaks of our need for the Spirit in the church. But the focus on Holy Laughter, on being drunk in the Spirit, on people who are glued to the floor, or on those who are struck dumb adds up to too much attention, to the neglect of obedience to the more important and crucial elements of Spirit life. This theme will be explored more fully in the last chapter.

Five

The Manifest Presence of Christ?

The Toronto Blessing would be no serious problem for most critics were it not for the strange manifestations that are a constant in the renewal. In this chapter we will examine in detail various defenses of these controversial "signs and wonders." Several caveats are in order before we examine the pro position.

(1) Defenders of the manifestations should consider a deeper and more rigorous study of them than we have seen up to now. I first heard this idea from Todd Hunter, National Coordinator of Vineyard Churches. Initially I was somewhat skeptical, but I now realize that he was on to something important about a proper analysis of the manifestations. Since many of the testimonies used to buttress their authenticity have been gathered quickly, with little probing at deeper levels of psychological and spiritual life, a more extensive and long-range study would help.

(2) All of the popular and controversial manifestations associated with The Toronto Blessing are not strictly miraculous in nature. Therefore, it is somewhat misleading for them to be so easily identified as "signs and wonders." There are ways, of course, that purely natural events or actions can legitimately be interpreted as miraculous. However, defenders of The Toronto Blessing should give more reflection to the fact that the manifestations do not easily fall under the category of miracle.

(3) Finally, defenders of The Toronto Blessing should be willing to rethink their endorsement of the respective manifestations. In my opinion, there would be far less concern about the Vineyard's latest phase if there were more caution about some of the more bizarre and extreme manifestations.

Description of the Manifestations

Many people have interpreted the Airport Vineyard meetings as the duplication of a typical Pentecostal or charismatic meeting. In large part this is a legitimate view, at least one heading in the right direction. However, even many Pentecostals have been shocked by some of the manifestations exhibited at The Toronto Blessing, and for those from noncharismatic backgrounds, there can be even greater discomfort.

At a typical evening rally, during ministry time (i.e., the last part of worship), you can expect to see a large number in the crowd "slain" in the Spirit (this is also known as "resting" in the Spirit). People simply fall backwards, allegedly under the power of the Holy Spirit. Such behavior has been common in Pentecostal and charismatic meetings as well as in Vineyard worship over the years.

Some people also dance at this point during the worship. Again, this is no new development, though an aesthetic distinction can easily be made between those who are naturally gifted or trained in liturgical dance versus those who distract worship by their clumsy, heavy-footed attempts.

Occasionally, one or two people will run during the service; these are sometimes called "Jesus laps." During one service in Long Island, one heavy-set woman did a lap, followed by a young man who could have run in the Olympics. The two of them almost collided when their paths crossed in one of the middle aisles.

Weeping is also common at Airport Vineyard meetings. Obviously for people who are dealing with emotional pain or spiritual problems, tears are an appropriate response to their inner needs. The weeping can also be a signal of repentance. Such crying has been common in churches with revival traditions. This, of course, is partial evidence against the view that there is no concern about sin in The Toronto Blessing.

One of the more controversial signs is the Holy Laughter. People laugh during various parts of worship, and this powerful experience of laughter can sweep the entire crowd, even during the preaching time. Several times the preaching at the Airport Vineyard has been stopped or cut short because of the pervasiveness of the laughter. One woman records what happened to her and a friend in these words:

> We burst into uncontrollable laughter. It overwhelmed us and we just howled with laughter. No matter how hard we tried, we couldn't stop—it was totally out of our control. . . . My girlfriend was lying across the seats and crawling along them like a worm, laughing hysterically and trying to get away from me. . . . To us it seemed that there was a wall of silence around us; we could see someone speaking, but we couldn't hear him. It was as if we were at our very own little party. . . . That evening my friend and I decided to go back—this time we wore ski pants![1]

Other manifestations have caused even greater bewilderment. For example, many people in worship engage in high-speed shaking of their hands, arms, or head. Others make various chopping and swinging motions. Such actions can take place at various times in the evening meetings. People so engaged may be seated, standing, or lying on the ground.

Still others have roared like lions or barked like dogs. I have personally heard both in various meetings. I also heard one man making noises like a cow. Others have reported people oinking like pigs and crowing like roosters. These animal noises have created the most disgust among some critics. As noted earlier, the dog barking has been linked historically with a famous Kentucky revival, while the lion roaring is said to be a prophetic action to signal a powerful word from Jesus, the lion of the tribe of Judah.

Frequent examples are also cited of people drunk in the Spirit. At several Airport meetings in January, 1995, people gathered to watch a man from Liverpool who was said to be "drunk as a skunk."

One or two people held him up while he prayed over others. I heard him warn one person not to fall on top of another, saying, "I may be drunk, but I do want to follow safety regulations." Several churches experiencing such manifestations even have designated drivers to take the drunk people home after worship.

There are also accounts of people becoming spiritually drunk at home, at work, or even while driving. Guy Chevreau, for example, tells the story of his wife, Janis, under God's power at one worship service; she continued in a stupor for forty-eight hours. He writes:

> At times [she was] unable to walk a straight line, certainly unfit to drive, or to host the guests that came for dinner the next evening. . . . There was no food in sight, and when I asked after the meal, Janis nearly fell to the floor in hysterical laughter. I went out to buy fish and chips. On my return, our guests were already seated at the table. Without any place settings, Janis proceeded to toss hot, greasy fish to each of us; she dumped the box of french fries in the middle of the table, and then pushed little piles in our respective directions, all the while finding everything very funny.[2]

Examples of such alleged Spirit-anointing explain why Randy Clark had one business card that read, "Bartender at Joel's Place." As noted earlier, this is also part of the background behind Rodney Howard-Browne calling himself "The Holy Ghost Bartender."

The Argument from Spiritual Renewal

Several lines of argument have been used to defend the various manifestations, even though the apologists agree that such actions seem bizarre on the surface. Chevreau admits that these "are unsettling, leaving many feeling that they have no grid for evaluation, no map to guide."[3] Dave Roberts acknowledges in his book that "even the most liberated charismatic" finds some of the manifestations difficult to accept.[4]

Some of the rationale given by various defenders deserves serious consideration. The primary argument is that God uses the manifestations to sanctify Christians and to convert unbelievers. For example, English pastor Dave Holden writes, "When we pray for [those at the meetings,] they laugh or weep. In the following days they talk of a sense of God's presence, their marriages being different, ethical change in their lives. We have discovered a new lease on life. Our prayer meetings have quadrupled."[5] John Arnott told me in an interview that this renewal has produced "the best Christian faith" he has ever seen. And a report from England reads:

> We have seen people whom we have counselled for years changed almost overnight. . . . The left hand of biblical counselling has been complemented by the right hand of God's power. People who were full of fear or self-imposed restrictions have changed. They're not like they were eight months ago.[6]

Faith Today, Canada's evangelical news magazine, in a cover story on The Toronto Blessing, cited Dr. Grant Mullen, a specialist in mood disorders at the Orchardview Medical Centre in Grimsby, Ontario, who was "excited about the emotional healing" at the Vineyard. He stated: "I've seen powerful psychological changes take place spontaneously that could never happen with years of counselling."[7]

In *Charisma*'s recent cover story, Eleanor Mumford, credited with introducing The Toronto Blessing to England, asserts: "What matters is what Jesus is doing in our bodies and our souls, in our hearts and our spirits."[8] The wife of a Vineyard pastor in southern England, she came to Toronto in the spring of 1994 during what was for her a time of spiritual depression. She testified at London's Holy Trinity Brompton Church that she had a deep encounter with Jesus while at the Airport Vineyard.

Such reports of emotional and spiritual renewal in the name of Jesus deserve great respect. They should serve as grounds to dismiss the view that The Toronto Blessing is totally wrong. Who can speak against such wonderful reports? We should praise God for the significant inner renewal and conversions that have resulted from The Toronto Blessing.

This line of argument, however, is not as simple as some Vineyard apologists propose. The fact that thousands receive emotional and spiritual help does not necessarily endorse the manifestations per se, especially the more bizarre ones. Consider the issue of some-one barking like a dog during worship. If asked about its meaning and value, that person will reply that the Holy Spirit is leading him or her to bark and through that to inner release and renewal. This kind of explanation has been accepted at Vineyard meetings.

But consider the person mentioned earlier who not only barked like a dog but also lifted up his leg to pretend to urinate. John Arnott rightly objected to the latter behavior, but surely the man could say that the Spirit led him both to bark and to pretend to urinate. On what grounds is he to be disciplined? If Vineyard leaders reply that this behavior is gross, what about the argument that people barking like dogs is also disgusting? We are, after all, talking about worship in the presence of God!

What needs focus here is the price paid when the Vineyard and other churches open the door to certain manifestations. Even the less radical "signs" have their problematic side. Consider men and women doing "carpet time" together, under great strains of moan-ing, screaming and holy laughing, each touching the other in fresh jolts from the Spirit. Or, picture a man who, after a round of carpet time and bouncing up and down like a pogo stick, is anointed by two women, with every touch of their hands (on his head, chest, legs, and feet) causing a fresh spasm of Spirit power as he is backed against a wall. While such behavior is not the norm, I have seen such actions on several occasions, sometimes even involving mem-bers of the Vineyard "ministry team" who are on duty.

The leap from manifestation to blessing is often greater than Vineyard apologists imagine. There needs to be more discernment in the monitoring of such signs and wonders. Simple acceptance of self-justifying explanations may not do for the extreme cases. At times some people have wanted to receive prayer at the Airport Vineyard but were prevented by the wild, uncontrollable actions of those around them.

The above cautions do not negate the value of the argument from spiritual and emotional renewal, especially as this applies to manifestations like weeping and laughter or even being slain in the

Spirit. But even here Vineyard leaders need to think more clearly about their rhetoric. For example, Randy Clark said at a "Catch the Fire" conference that those under the anointing should make sure they have someone to catch them. He recalled one lady in Florida who did not heed that warning. When the Holy Spirit came on her, she fell backwards, hit her head on a concrete wall, and landed in the hospital for a week. Is this really to be attributed to God? At Toronto meetings several people have fallen on top of others during the power encounters with the Spirit, resulting in cuts and bruises. Do we credit this to the Spirit as he anoints the faithful?

Weaker Arguments for the Manifestations

In any controversy, both legitimate and questionable arguments are advanced in favor of given views. Some of the points used to defend the manifestations are weaker than the primary argument just mentioned about personal and spiritual renewal.

Sandy Millar, the vicar of Holy Trinity Brompton, contends that Christian critics do not even have the insight of some of the unsaved. Speaking of manifestations, he stated: "The nonbelievers usually think it's fine. They think if there is a God, then he's likely to act in unusual ways."[9] One wonders how wide a sample of unbelievers Millar has queried about the wild shaking, twitching, dog barking, and lion roaring. Also, suppose these people thought such actions were "crazy"; would he still trust their judgment? Or does he cite them simply because they happen to agree with his view?

The point is frequently made that the media coverage of The Toronto Blessing has been gentle—an observation that has been used to give credibility to the renewal. No doubt there are reporters impressed by what is happening. However, many secular media people I have interviewed think that the manifestations are better understood as signals of mass hysteria and deep emotional release than as supernatural acts of God.

Apologists also use an argument about humility to defend the renewal. The fact that the movement is supposed to involve "nameless" and "faceless" leaders is stressed. However, John Wimber and

Rodney Howard-Browne are not exactly unknown figures. Rather, they are the two major international leaders behind "Holy Laughter." Likewise, Randy Clark, who was anointed by Rodney Howard-Browne, is now known around the charismatic world. Local Vineyard leaders, John and Carol Arnott, have no end to worldwide invitations.

There is nothing intrinsically wrong with any of this. I have personally found each of these leaders to be humble and approachable. But this reality does not prove that the manifestations are from God. Conversely, the fact that the famous critics of The Toronto Blessing are humble or godly people does not prove their allegations to be valid either.

Consider the case of R. T. Kendall, pastor of Westminster Chapel, who has stated that participation in the "manifestations" can be humbling. Regarding his own experience he said:

> I think God was wanting to teach me to be humbled, to look stupid and to be a fool. There I was, on the floor in front of all my deacons and their wives. There were only a couple of others to whom it happened that evening and I was embarrassed. I think that was what God wanted to do to me.[10]

Kendall, of course, must be given the benefit of the doubt in telling about his own experience and what it meant for him. However, this kind of reasoning is sometimes used to make the larger point that critics of the rather bizarre manifestations simply lack humility and are unwilling to look foolish. What must be remembered is the crucial distinction that may exist between being a "fool for Christ" versus simply engaging in foolish behavior.

There is also a fundamental contradiction in the rhetoric about the manifestations. It is said night after night in Toronto that they are not important. Yet those who do not fall down or display some other sign are told that they have the HTR condition—that is, "Hard To Receive." If manifestations are secondary, why all the fuss? According to one report, a youth pastor in Toronto who did not fall when she received prayer was told to fall down anyway.

Ron Allen of the Fort Wayne Vineyard states: "Our meetings are messy and a little scary, but then we've moved from the order of respectability to the order of anointing."[11] Should there not be more concern about "messy" and "scary" meetings? Must it be so easily defended by an exaggerated dichotomy between anointing and respectability?

There needs to be deeper reflection on the attribution of the Spirit's work in charismatic worship. At Airport Vineyard meetings, the Spirit allegedly moves so freely that all it takes for some to fall over, laugh, writhe on the floor, twitch, or shake is a simple hand motion from someone in leadership. Or, for others, a leader may wave the Spirit towards them or simply blow on them. Can the Holy Spirit be so easily dispensed? Some Vineyard leaders have taken my query here to be unwillingness to allow the Spirit liberty. That criticism must be taken seriously since Scripture says, "Since we live by the Spirit, let us keep in step with the Spirit" (Gal. 5:25). Nevertheless, I think extreme behavior in Vineyard worship may not be "in step with the Spirit." The Spirit may be quenched by falsely crediting human acts to him, and that deserves criticism as well.

From the same angle, proponents of The Toronto Blessing frequently complain about the theological traditions that put God in a box. However, this sword cuts both ways. Surely Pentecostals, charismatics, and those in the Third Wave are also adept at allowing their theology to hamper the work of the Spirit.

This point has been missed by William DeArteaga in his popular work, *Quenching the Spirit*. He naively assumes that discernment of the Spirit is to be equated with basic Pentecostal theology. That perspective enables him to make absurd statements like, "The Reformers rejected the need for discernment when they threw out the whole of Catholic mystical theology."[12] What will Calvin scholars make of this judgment: "Calvin's expanded cessationism unintentionally destroyed the capacity for spiritual discernment in Reformed Protestantism"?[13]

One of DeArteaga's chapters makes the astounding argument that cessationism led directly to the destruction of Christianity in northern Europe. He argues that Hume's famous essay against miracles was easily victorious because Protestants had long given up on the supernatural. This simplistic reading of intellectual thought fails on at least two counts. (1) The temporary success of the Enlightenment had more to do with complex issues in epistemology than with the matter of cessationism. By the time of Hume, theological stability had been rocked by two centuries of debate over trusting religious authorities, Scripture, sense data, rationalism, and common beliefs. (2) The philosophy of David Hume was so tightly skeptical that he argues that miracles can *never* prove religion. In other words, the presence of miracle-working Pentecostals may have had no impact on him.[14]

It is also disconcerting how readily DeArteaga pins the label "Pharisee" on Christian thinkers and traditions. This move has been adopted in defense of The Toronto Blessing. Consider the way Guy Chevreau equates opposition to this renewal movement as parallel to the conversion of Saul.

> He was the equivalent of a tenured position at the local seminary; his theology was circumscribed and systematic; he knew what he knew, and he knew what wasn't of God when he saw it . . . until he got knocked off his high horse. The manifest presence of the Risen Christ undid him thoroughly![15]

Although there are good arguments for being open to The Toronto Blessing, its leading defenders sound like Pharisees themselves when they resort to name-calling against fellow Christians. Likewise, the parallels between endorsing The Toronto Blessing and Saul's experience on the road to Damascus may be worth exploring, but such comparisons do not warrant the simplistic dismissal of the real and critical questions about the problematic aspects of the former.

Where Is Jonathan Edwards When You Need Him?

One of the great ironies in the controversy about Holy Laughter and The Toronto Blessing is the appeal to Jonathan Edwards from *both* critics *and* defenders. It is unfortunate that Edwards, the great American philosopher and revivalist, is no longer able to speak for himself. Likewise, we have all sorts of conflicting claims about what John Wesley and Charles Finney would have thought about Holy Laughter and The Toronto Blessing.

Guy Chevreau devotes one-third of his work *Catch the Fire* to a study of Jonathan Edwards. Because Guy's doctoral work was in historical theology, focusing on Edwards is not surprising. Also, who better to turn to for support of The Toronto Blessing than to a man whose name is synonymous with renewal and revival?

I have read through the book carefully, reviewing many parts several times. At first, I felt somewhat at loss in his long chapter on Edwards. I had never done a special study of this great preacher or of the Great Awakening, so I was not sure of the overall context and background to Guy's summary and application. But some of the high points of Chevreau's argument must be noted. He begins his chapter on Edwards with a personal confession:

> Mid-February, while sitting on the floor during one of the ministry times at the Airport Vineyard, I surveyed the bodies laid out everywhere, and leaned over to a newly-made friend and said, "All of this makes applesauce of a fellow's theological applecarts."[16]

Guy turns to Jonathan Edwards to help sort out the applesauce.

The first section of the chapter offers extensive quotations from Edwards and his wife Sarah about their experiences of spiritual ecstasy. After these lengthy descriptions, Edwards is quoted as saying:

> Now if these things are enthusiasm, and the fruits of a distempered brain, let my brain be evermore possessed of that happy distemper. If this be distraction, I pray God that the world of mankind may all be seized with this benign, meek, beneficent, beautiful, glorious distraction![17]

Chevreau then makes this comparison: "While the manifestations may be new to many of us, they are not untypical experiences when the Spirit of God comes to renew His people."[18] This, of course, is a misleading judgment. Many of the manifestations connected with The Toronto Blessing were *not* experienced during Edwards' day. Likewise, rounds of Holy Laughter did not interrupt his preaching!

I do not dispute the central premise behind Chevreau's citations from Edwards and his wife. He, like Edwards, wants Christians to be receptive and open to powerful moves of the Holy Spirit—a point well taken. But that is far different from his equation of the Great Awakening with the assortment of manifestations currently under debate.

Chevreau then draws a further comparison between the past renewal and our time. He notes that the "timeless spirit of judgmentalism and fault-finding seemed to have been as unfettered in Edwards' day as many currently experience it."[19] Later, he introduces us to Charles Chauncy (1705–87), the famous opponent of Edwards and author of the notorious work *Enthusiasm Described and Caution'd Against* (1742). Chevreau pictures Chauncy as a rather dense and pathetic figure, caught in the chains of a theology of "Father, Son and Holy Book."[20] With this latter jab, Chevreau even states that Chauncy "concludes his instruction [against enthusiasm] with this myopic assertion: 'Let us fetch our notions of religion from the Scripture.'"[21] While Guy has every right to question Chauncy's *interpretation* of Scripture, Chauncy's respect for the *authority* of Scripture deserves no ridicule.

Chevreau's points here are misleading, not only about history, but also as a guide to the debate today. The "timeless spirit of judgmentalism and fault-finding" showed no favoritism in the Great Awakening. *Both* critics *and* defenders were adept at mean-spirited, picky, and absurd judgments. If Chauncy erred in this regard as a critic, then Gilbert Tennent (1703–64), a defender of the "New Light," can be cited for the same arrogance. His famous sermon on "The Danger of an Unconverted Ministry" (preached on March 8, 1740) is as mean and judgmental as anything one will read in Chauncy.[22]

Chevreau states that "it is of note that later in his life, Chauncy gave leadership to the Unitarians."[23] Chevreau cites William DeArteaga's work *Quenching the Spirit* as his source, and there is no doubt that Chauncy became more liberal in his theology.[24] What Chevreau and DeArteaga need to be careful of here is drawing the inference that Chauncy's liberalism stemmed from his opposition to Edwards' revivalism. It seems more likely is that it originated in Chauncy's objection to Edwards' Calvinism!

Consider this evaluation from the great historian Sydney Ahlstrom. After referring to battles over Calvinism, he writes:

> Such contention had serious negative consequences, in that it drove many peace-loving souls out of the churches and led many more to embrace milder forms of religion. The Great Awakening thus became the single most important catalyst of [the] "Arminian" tradition which had been growing surreptitously and half-consciously since the turn of the century.[25]

Chevreau's complaints about past "judgmentalism and fault-finding" is a useful sword to wield against current critics. However, again, this sword is two-edged. The defenders of today's alleged renewal are, in my opinion, as adept as their ancestors in arrogance and mean-spiritedness. What could be more unspiritual than the divine threats from alleged prophets that have been issued against fellow Christians who question the negative aspects of Holy Laughter and The Toronto Blessing?

Many of the other points raised by Chevreau from Edwards are legitimate in themselves, but their application to The Toronto Blessing is still up for debate. For example, who today would doubt Edwards' view that "God is further from confining Himself to a particular method in His work on souls, than some imagine"?[26] Likewise, consider this quotation from Edwards:

> The Holy Spirit is sovereign in His operation; and we know that He uses a great variety; and we cannot tell how great a variety He may use, within the compass of the rules He Himself has fixed. We ought not to limit God where He has not limited Himself.[27]

This is an obvious axiom for a Christian, but it does not settle whether Christians today should allow themselves to bark like dogs or shake for hours or interrupt preaching with rounds of laughter.

Chevreau goes on to cite Edwards as a warning to those who are waiting to make up their mind about The Toronto Blessing. Since this argument is now being used repeatedly, it is worth citing the long relevant passage from Edwards.

> It is probable that many of those who are thus waiting, know not for what they are waiting. If they wait to see a work of God without difficulties, and stumbling blocks, it will be like the fool's waiting at the river side to have the water all run by.
>
> This pretended prudence, in persons waiting so long before they acknowledge this work, will probably in the end prove the greatest imprudence. Hereby they will fail of any share of so great a blessing, and will miss the most precious opportunity of obtaining divine light, grace, and comfort, heavenly and eternal benefits that God ever gave in **New England**.
>
> While the glorious fountain is set open in so wonderful a manner, and while multitudes flock to it and receive a rich supply for the want of their souls, they stand at a distance, doubting, wondering, and receiving nothing, and are like to continue thus till the precious season is past.[28]

I have put the words "New England" in bold since the initial point to make is the obvious one. Jonathan Edwards is *not* writing about Toronto, and we do *not* know if he would have applied this verdict to our time. I suggest that Edwards' Calvinism, his high regard for intellectual and theological analysis, and his esteem for careful, biblical preaching would have led him to have some serious hesitations about Holy Laughter and The Toronto Blessing.

More important, there is something disconcerting about Edwards' verdict, even for his own day. His powerful rhetoric should not cloud a fundamental confusion on his part. Beneath his proper call for a decision about the gospel, he also forced his hearers to choose sides on secondary items. It simply did not occur to him that the Holy Spirit could work outside of the parameters of the revival Edwards worked so hard to explain and defend. In other words, against his own theological advice, he put God in a box. In Chevreau's terms, Edwards had his own "theological applecarts" that deserved to be upset.

Chevreau also quotes Edwards on this point: "To rejoice that the work of God is carried on calmly, without much ado, is in effect to rejoice that it is carried on with less power, or that there is not so much of the influence of God's Spirit."[29] For a philosopher who usually offers profound and discriminating analysis, this point is naive even in the way that he applies it to the multitudes. The simplistic equation of calmness with less Spirit power should be resisted by those who know the God who says: "Be still, and know that I am God" (Ps. 46:10).

There is one final comment from Edwards that deserves profound attention, as it applies equally to his day and ours. In a section on "one cause of errors attending a great revival of religion," he writes:

> The first and the worst cause of errors, that prevail in such a state of things, is *spiritual pride*. This is the main door by which the devil comes into the hearts of those who are zealous for the advancement of religion. This is the main handle by which the devil has hold of religious persons, and the chief source of all the mischief that he introduces, to clog and hinder a work of God.[30]

Several general observations can conclude this study of the use of Edwards. Guy Chevreau's account in *Catch the Fire* is to be applauded more for its faithful summary of Edwards than for its careful application of Edwards concerning The Toronto Blessing. This same point has been made forcefully by Iain H. Murray, one of the great scholars on Edwards, who writes in an important review of Chevreau's book.

> It must be said that the long treatment of the thought of Jonathan Edwards is, in our judgment, well and fairly done. No one could read that chapter without profit. It is also clear that the author, who writes with an appealing sincerity, has absorbed some of Edwards' main emphases and in particular the point that

physical actions can never of themselves provide any proof of the power of the Holy Spirit.

But while asserting this, Guy Chevreau contradicts it by constructing his book very largely *around* the physical phenomenon. We fail to see how this is consistent with what he quotes from Edwards. If physical pheneomena, such as falling down, are not *the* vital thing, why should they be given such prominence? We can understand secular reporters giving all their attention to the merely outward, but this book appears to confirm that those most closely involved are themselves far too interested in the appearance of things.

It is true that far too much evangelical religion, not least in North America, has been seriously devoid of emotion and spiritual fire. But the great danger of this book is that, perhaps unwittingly, it gives the impresssion that our current is not so much for the great central truths of the gospel as it is for the kind of phenemena which it does so much to bring to the attention of people around the world.[31]

It is also useful to realize a major difficulty that we face when we make historical judgments. When Todd Hunter, National Coordinator of Vineyard Churches, asked me once about the use of Edwards in defense of The Toronto Blessing, I had two replies. It certainly does not hurt the Vineyard to cite Edwards as an ally. All things being equal, I think that Edwards would have some sympathy for The Toronto Blessing. But I also told Todd that it was tough enough to try and figure out what is going on in our day among people we can actually meet, without undue attention being paid to the proper interpretation of complex renewals from the past.

In the end, we must each do our own analysis and not be too burdened by the ghosts of Edwards or Chauncy.

John Wimber's Response

In his "Leadership Letter" of July-August, 1994, John Wimber responded to the issues related to The Toronto Blessing.[32] I will note some of his comments and give a brief reply. It is not hard to detect a certain hesitation about different aspects of the latest Vineyard developments, and Wimber's approach to the manifestations is certainly more balanced than that of many in the Vineyard.

Wimber: "We love to read and hear about revival. But going through the birthing process of revival is very much like the birth of a child: messy." (p. 1)

Comment: This is an interesting analogy, but it must not be overworked. After all, some elements of the birthing process can be dangerous to a baby's health. It is also interesting that Wimber used this analogy when he embraced the prophetic in 1988.[33]

Wimber: "Gamaliel stepped in to offer his wise advice: 'Leave these men alone! Let them go! For if their purpose or activity is of human origin, it will fail. But if it is from God, you will not be able to stop these men; you will only find yourselves fighting against God' (Acts 5:38–39)." (p. 2)

Comment: Though Gamaliel's words are in the Bible, this does not make his view as a Jewish leader equal to apostolic teaching. Gamaliel's advice is partially misleading. There are many non-Christian or anti-Christian messages that thrive over hundreds of years. Consider, for example, the spread of Islam or the dominance of secular humanism. Of course, his warning against "fighting against God" is apt.

Wimber: "I trust God entirely. . . . It's human beings that concern me. That doesn't mean we have to expel every little thing that doesn't have a proof text. For the time being, we can leave a few things in the file folder labeled 'I don't know.'" (p. 3)

Comment: Wimber's ease with ambiguity is a decent trait. His concern over the human factor is crucial in responding to The Toronto Blessing. The ease with which the human factor distorts God's work is something that needs focus, especially in a renewal when God gets credited with everything.

Wimber: "Neither I nor the Bible equate phenomena such as falling, shaking, crying out, laughing or making animal noises with an experience with God. However, you can have an experience with God that may result in some of those responses." (p. 5)

Comment: The distinction Wimber makes is important, though I personally think that the "animal noises" deserve a great deal more suspicion in the Vineyard.

Wimber: "So if someone comes to me after they've shaken, fallen down, or made a noise, my question is, 'Do you love Jesus more? Do you believe in him more? Are you committed to him?' If the answer is 'Yes!' then praise the Lord!" (p. 6)

Comment: Wimber's previously noted concerns about the human element should make him more cautious. As The Toronto Blessing sweeps the globe, the willing multitudes are being taught this as the standard defense to the manifestations. This too readily opens the door to the chaotic forces of human emotions and religious ecstasy. After barking like a dog in public, who is going to be self-critical and say that he or she does not feel closer to Jesus?

Wimber: "Let's not get distracted with the overzealous activity of some, but keep our focus on the main and plain things of Scripture. In other words, let's begin organizing ourselves to give this blessing away." (p. 7)

Comment: There is no task more serious than for apologists of The Toronto Blessing to listen closely to Wimber in his biblical and missionary thrust. This same spirit was captured in the Vineyard Board's report from a meeting called by Wimber in September, 1994. Writing on behalf of his colleagues, Todd Hunter, National Coordinator, noted:

> It is our desire to embrace all that is good about this renewal while correcting that which is excessive, long-term hurtful or contrary to biblical mandates. . . . We are committed to "power evangelism," not just "power"; we are committed to "signs and wonders and church growth," not just "signs and wonders."[34]

Six
Lying Signs and Wonders?

Critics of The Toronto Blessing have wasted no time in focusing on the manifestations as a central weakness. In this chapter we will examine the arguments of several of the major critics. Though some of them overlap, they have argued against The Toronto Blessing along diverse lines.

Two preliminary observations are in order. (1) I would urge Vineyard members and proponents of Holy Laughter not to dismiss any of their critics out of hand. John MacArthur, Hank Hanegraaff, and other critics have wide and varied ministries. While they may have made mistakes in one area, that does not require us to refuse to hear anything else from them. Someone may be wrong on some issues but still have the mind of Christ on others.

(2) It is not helpful to dismiss such critics as simply "unspiritual." After all, being spiritual covers a whole range of factors. In fact, anyone who has been justified by faith in Christ is spiritual (Eph. 1:3). The serious issues raised by critics must not be dismissed with such *ad hominem* judgments.

The Criticisms of John MacArthur

John MacArthur is no stranger to controversy. In recent years he has been involved in disputes over evangelical dialogue with Catholics, the relationship of faith and works, and criticism of charismatics. My concern is with this last category.

There was a time when I tended to dismiss MacArthur's well-known work *Charismatic Chaos*. That book is, in fact, marred by unfair statements and numerous examples of sloppy logic. The book also has a bitter edge. One subtitle, for example, speaks of charismatics as "Keen but Clueless."[1] Is such language really necessary from one Christian to another? His polemical style hurt the chances of the book being heard by charismatics, though it is a favored book among anticharismatics.

Over the last couple of years, however, I have developed a greater appreciation for the book simply because I have seen more and more chaos in the charismatic world. Whatever weaknesses *Charismatic Chaos* exhibits, MacArthur is on to something of significance that should disturb charismatics more than anyone else. They may not appreciate the book, but they do need to do a better job of monitoring a chaotic theology and style that rightly disturbs any Christian.

MacArthur's objections to the Vineyard's latest trend appears in his most recent work, *Reckless Faith*,[2] in which he warns of several trends that show "a loss of will to discern" in the church. He targets Holy Laughter and The Toronto Blessing along several lines. I will quote from MacArthur and then respond, based on my own research and analysis.

MacArthur: "This is pure mysticism, rooted in feeling but devoid of any cognitive element. The worshiper sees the mystical 'emotive event' divorced from any objective truth as an encounter with God." (p. 156)

Response: True, the Holy Laughter revival is partly mystical and rooted in feeling. But the encounters are not "devoid of any cognitive element," nor is the mystical event "divorced from any objective truth." These experiences are rooted in Christian worship and obedience to biblical faith.

MacArthur: "Crowds in excess of a thousand people gather nightly for meetings where paroxysms of laughter constitute the order of service." (p. 156)

Response: This may give a false impression that the laughter dominates every service. In fact, outbreaks of Holy Laughter die out and are not the whole story. Media clips often focus on the strange manifestations in the long worship services and give a false picture of their pervasiveness.

MacArthur: MacArthur tells the story of Randy Clark, who initially objected to God's leading for him to go to a Word Faith church to hear Rodney Howard-Browne. Clark stated: "The Lord spoke to me immediately, and said, 'You have a denominational spirit. How badly do you want to be touched afresh?'"

To this MacArthur comments: "So the theological differences Randy Clark was willing to overlook for the sake of the experience he was seeking are no mere trifles. Note that it was not a rational understanding of any truth, but the phenomena—people shaking, falling, laughing—that convinced Clark this was what he needed." (pp. 157–58)

Response: I agree with MacArthur that Randy Clark and other Vineyard leaders should be wary of their associations with the Word Faith tradition. Since this movement is dealt with elsewhere in chapter 4, I will not add more. However, Clark's intent was not to join a Word Faith church but simply to hear Rodney Howard-Browne at the Rhema Church in Tulsa. While Rodney preaches in Word Faith churches, he cannot be accurately described, in my opinion, as a typical Word Faith preacher. In fact, as noted earlier, Rodney prefers to see himself as an "old-time Pentecostal."

Finally, it is misleading to imply that Clark was simply after experience. He wanted spiritual renewal. Likewise, he was not impressed by the shaking, falling, and laughing per se, but by the inner healing that his friends told him accompanied such manifestations.

MacArthur: "But the laughing revival is simply not concerned with doctrinal issues. It has already crossed all denominational boundaries from the most formal high-church Anglicanism to the most outlandish charismatic sects. And it has done so precisely because it has nothing whatever to do with objective truth. It is all about sensation, emotion, and feeling good." (p. 158)

Response: These are misleading generalizations. The leaders of the "laughing revival" are concerned about doctrine and care about biblical teaching. The spread of Holy Laughter has more to do with Christians of all persuasions reaching out to God than it does with something that has "nothing whatever to do with objective truth."

MacArthur: "Now God is in the hands of a giddy mob—or so the mob thinks. . . . Instead of true, abiding joy, they had settled for sheer bedlam." (p. 172)

Response: MacArthur is properly worried about the dangers of wild and chaotic worship. That legitimate concern is only marred by his pejorative description of fellow Christians as a "giddy mob," who care only about "sheer bedlam" rather than "true, abiding joy." This may be true of some, but it is an unfair and extreme reaction.

MacArthur: "How can a movement stoked by the heat of raw passion rekindle the flames when people's emotions finally grow cold?" (p. 174)

Response: MacArthur is legitimately concerned about the "valley" low that often follows the "mountain" high of ecstatic worship. Of course, the rhetorical question can be answered by hoping that Toronto Blessing recipients will pursue daily obedience to Jesus, deep study in the Word, and continual worship in a local fellowship.

Concerns from Hank Hanegraaff

Hank Hanegraaff is president of the Christian Research Institute in southern California, following Walter Martin as head of the evangelical world's largest anticult organization. He is also host of "The Bible Answer Man" and author of *Christianity in Crisis*, the blockbuster critique of the Word of Faith movement.

In a telephone interview I asked Hank if he thought the Vineyard had become a cult. He replied "Absolutely not!" Nevertheless, he has grave concerns about Holy Laughter and The Toronto Blessing. In a taped message he states that Howard-Browne's ministry and The Toronto Blessing amounts to "counterfeit revival" with "lying signs and wonders." These are strong words.

As with MacArthur, Hank's concerns will be listed and my response follows. I will also interact with Richard Riss, a historian of revivals, who is circulating an unpublished rejoinder to Hanegraaff's tape under the title "The Counterfeit Revival?"

Hanegraaff: Toronto Blessing preachers who predict a great revival as an event just prior to the return of Christ are mistaken. "In biblical eschatology, the precursor to the coming of the Lord is great apostasy."[3] Hank hints that this "counterfeit revival" may have links with such apostasy.

Response: On this issue, Riss argues that the popular idea of a great apostasy is only a recent teaching in the church and states that Jonathan Edwards believed in a coming revival. Who is right: Riss or Hanegraaff?

Hanegraaff's point is about biblical eschatology, not about history, and Riss has neglected to reply with Scripture. Furthermore, Riss is on slippery ground historically. Apocalyptic warnings of apostasy were popular in the early church, among key leaders in the Middle Ages, during Reformation times, and even among some in Edwards' day.[4] Furthermore, it is ironic that those who now announce the coming revival also circulate the popular prophecy books announcing the coming apostasy. The Airport Vineyard has a whole shelf of such books. This kind of prophetic double-talk is confusing.

Hanegraaff's biblical argument, however, only speaks against those who argue for the intimate connection of revival and the Second Coming. One could hope, as he does, for real revival in the church without contradicting the popular premillennial view of prophecy.[5]

Hanegraaff: The "awful, devilish manifestations" that take place should be monitored better. Wimber's "wait and see" attitude about the extreme manifestations is "a far cry from a pastor protecting his sheep against wolves."

Response: For background, one should know that Wimber used to interpret some of the manifestations as demonic. Wimber, of course, has a right to change his mind. But he remains concerned about some of the manifestations. As noted earlier, his assessment has been far more cautious than many other Vineyard leaders.

Riss critiques Hanegraaff by saying that the wolves that pastors are to guard against "are people, not manifestations." This is far too simplistic and shallow. Pastors are to protect the sheep from false teachers *and* false practices.

Hanegraaff: Holy Laughter and the other manifestations open a door into the occult.

Response: This is a version of the slippery slide argument. As noted in chapter 2, the validity of the argument depends on how slippery is the particular slide. I believe that the vast majority of people who have experienced The Toronto Blessing will never end up in the occult. Charismatics, Pentecostals, and Vineyard members live in a different universe from followers of the occult.

Hanegraaff: The manifestations of The Toronto Blessing are duplicated in Eastern religions and in the New Age movement.

Response: True, some of these manifestations can be found among Rajneesh followers or devotees of other gurus. What this may suggest more than anything is a psychological readiness of humans to display a wide range of behavior in worship when such opportunity is given.

Hanegraaff: The recent focus on being drunk in the Lord is a misinterpretation of Acts 2:1–13. That passage does not prove that the believers were acting drunk but that certain cynics (who "made fun of them," 2:13) misinterpreted the other languages at Pentecost as the babble of drunk people.

Response: Riss accuses Hanegraaff of "stretching things" and asks: "Where in the world would these witnesses get the idea that the apostles were drunk if they were only speaking in other tongues? Why would such a thing occur to them?" There is a simple answer to Riss. The doubters did not understand the "Babel" of languages being supernaturally spoken by disciples. Such a chorus of "tongues" would sound to any who did not understand them like drunken revelry. The ones amazed are those who actually heard their own foreign tongue being spoken by the Galileans, a group not known for their linguistic skills.[6]

Hanegraaff: "Paul, of course, is not saying that drunkenness is desirable and has some kind of a biblical counterpart."

Response: In our time, believers are duplicating drunkenness by staggering walk, faltering speech, and inability to stand. Designated drivers are chosen for those under the power of the new wine. God forbid the day when some Christian under the "anointing" causes serious harm through careless driving.

Again, Riss has an opposing view. He quotes Ephesians 5:18: "Do not get drunk on wine, which leads to debauchery. Instead, be filled with the Spirit." He then states: "This verse very clearly compares the effects of the Holy Spirit to the effects of alcohol." My exegetical sympathies are in favor of Hanegraaff's concern. Surely the dominant tradition in the church is that Paul is *contrasting* the effects of the Spirit with that of alcohol, not comparing them.

Granted, this alone will not decide what to make of the accounts of people who, drunk in the Spirit, report inner healing and spiritual renewal. However, the context of Ephesians 5:18 and the force of the passage itself suggests that Paul has in mind the *opposite* impact of old wine and Spirit-led behavior.

Hanegraaff: He expresses incredulity about reports that Smith Wigglesworth, an earlier Pentecostal leader, raised someone from the dead. He wonders why this was not "front page news."

Response: Riss replies by stating that he knows of "approximately twelve cases of resurrections from the dead in modern times," but the media were not willing to do anything about them. But given the sympathetic media treatment of The Toronto Blessing, perhaps Riss should run these accounts by reporters again. Failing that, Riss should do the Christian world a favor and provide evidence of these "well substantiated" accounts to *Christianity Today* or even to the *Journal* published by CRI.

Hanegraaff: "Past revivals were conducted in an atmosphere of reverential awe for God. Revival was constantly accompanied by the powerful proclamation of the Word of God. There was a conviction of sin and a desire for repentance."

Response: Speaking generally, these concerns are legitimate. There is not enough sense of reverence in Airport Vineyard meetings or enough focus on conviction of sin and the need for repentance. This, of course, is a matter of emphasis. Top Vineyard leaders have expressed concerns identical to those of Hanegraaff.

Hanegraaff: "They're coming into an experience, not the everlasting Savior."

Response: This is a false disjunction. Thousands who have come to The Toronto Blessing love Jesus and want an experience of encounter with Jesus. Whatever the weaknesses and excesses of their experiences, I believe the vast majority care to meet their everlasting Savior.

Hanegraaff: This is a counterfeit revival.

Response: As noted earlier, I share many of Hanegraaff's concerns about the Word Faith movement. We share the same concerns about the cults. We also agree on many of the weaknesses of The Toronto Blessing. It is out of this agreement that I say that Hanegraaff has overstated the case by using the phrase "counterfeit revival." Ironically, Vineyard leaders do not refer to The Toronto Blessing as a revival, though Rodney Howard-Browne refers to his work as a revival. In both cases, however, there is no necessity to speak of "counterfeit" or of "lying signs and wonders."

Conversely, Rodney Howard-Browne and some Vineyard leaders have used much more extreme language about Hanegraaff and his ministry. Moreover, some of the prominent Word Faith preachers have gone far beyond the bounds of Christian discourse in their arrogant rhetoric against both Hanegraaff and Walter Martin.

The Critique from Spiritual Counterfeits Project

Warren Smith wrote a strong criticism of The Toronto Blessing in the Fall, 1994, issue of the *SCP Newsletter*, entitled "Holy Laughter or Strong Delusion?" It is significant that this title offers a strong disjunction, one that in my opinion presents false options. The laughing renewal can be "holy" and contain some delusion, a mixture of Spirit and flesh. Polar opposite choices are often unproductive when examining complex realities.

Smith: "There is no biblical precedent for Holy Laughter."

Response: Granted, there is no powerful biblical case to be made for this modern phenomenon. However, laughter per se is not antibiblical.

Smith: "Substituting the word 'joy' for 'laughter' is a *non sequitur*. It is inaccurate and misleading."

Response: While Smith is technically right, I don't think Toronto Blessing advocates are trying to say that all joy must be expressed by laughter. They may simply be making the right and proper point that joy often leads to laughter.

Smith: "Holy Laughter advocates rarely, if ever, discuss the need to 'test the spirits.'"

Response: Smith's basic point here is simply false. Has he not read Guy Chevreau's in-depth analysis of Jonathan Edwards in the work *Catch the Fire*? John Arnott, the Airport Vineyard leader, has had years of involvement in deliverance ministry. John Wimber called an international summit of Vineyard leaders to work through the strange manifestations.

Smith tries to prove his point by quoting Charles and Frances Hunter's remark that one should "never question the way God does" things. That remark by the Hunters is legitimate. The disputed issue is sorting through what God does versus what people say that God does.

Smith: "Holy Laughter advocates rarely, if ever, talk about the Spirit's express warning that in the latter times some people will be supernaturally seduced by deceptive evil spirits into following them and not the one true God."

Response: Again, Smith is mistaken. While this modern renewal has a postmillennial flavor, I have heard many warnings from Vineyard preachers about last-day deceptions involving satanism, New Age, the cults in general, liberalism, or even dead conservative churches.

Smith: "Holy Laughter advocates rarely, if ever, talk about the Bible's warnings of false prophets who come in the name of Jesus but bring with them 'another spirit.'"

Response: Smith has not listened to enough Vineyard messages or sermons from Rodney Howard-Browne, for both camps offer warnings about such false prophets. At the Airport Vineyard bookstore is a whole section of material against such false prophets. The bookstore even stocks Walter Martin's classic work, *The Kingdom of the Cults.*

Smith: "Many laughter advocates condescendingly discourage and even openly intimidate sincere Christians who question the laughing revival. The Hunters' book *Holy Laughter* refers to skeptics as God's 'frozen chosen.'"

Response: Smith is correct here. This is the saddest and most pathetic aspect of the Holy Laughter movement. The advocates are either so pompous or so insecure that they regularly pronounce doom on any who question the manifestations. I find their prophetic pronouncements presumptuous.

Smith: "Holy Laughter advocates blatantly disregard the biblical admonition that things be done decently and in order."

Response: All things being equal, the chaos and confusion in many Vineyard meetings lends credence to Smith's concern. This will be examined more closely in the last section of this chapter.

Smith: "Laughter advocates rarely, if ever, discuss the well-documented demonic deceptions that have been manifested in past revivals."

Response: Vineyard leaders should be a little red-faced that their own teaching has reversed on what constitutes demonic behavior. However, teachers like Guy Chevreau and Richard Riss have dealt at length with all facets of past revivals, including the demonic. When Wimber was at the Airport Vineyard meeting in June, 1994, he dealt with a demonic spirit that he believed was present.

Smith: "The laughing revival could one day merge with what the New Age calls the coming day of 'planetary Pentecost.'"

Response: Yes, I suppose it could. And SCP "could" one day join the New Age as well. However, until either Vineyard leaders or SCP leaders show interest in the New Age, either possibility seems as unlikely as the Pope becoming a Southern Baptist. The Vineyard has regularly attacked the New Age movement, and the Airport Vineyard bookstore contains a good arsenal of books against the New Age movement.

Are Manifestations Secondary?

John Arnott and other Vineyard leaders must be exhausted at the constant barrage of questions about the manifestations. They repeatedly say that the manifestations are secondary. In my thirty or so visits to the Airport Vineyard I have heard this disclaimer repeatedly. So, why bother asking the question again?

The issue bears some further reflection for the simple reason that reality may be more complex than a simple answer implies, even a positive one. I am not accusing Arnott or any other Vineyard leader of lying or being deceptive. However, I think there are some key reasons to think that the manifestations are being given more prominence than some Vineyard leaders suggest.

Consider the origin of The Toronto Blessing. The reason why people hold the date of January 20, 1994, as special is because that is the night when the "manifestations" came to the Airport Vineyard. Within weeks the word was out in Toronto churches that something special was happening at the Vineyard. One chief element in the story was the presence of the manifestations, that the Holy Spirit was being poured out at the Airport Vineyard as evidenced by the falling, shaking, laughing, and so forth.

Recently I received a copy of Randy Clark's message that he delivered that first night. I had been told by various people that the outpouring of the Spirit was a complete surprise to Airport Vineyard people, an unexpected move of God. But Clark's message should have prepared anyone present for the arrival of the manifestations. He gave a dramatic account of his own experience of the manifestations under the ministry of Rodney Howard-Browne.

Thus, when Randy extended an invitation that night for "ministry," the people knew what was involved.

Some reflection should also be given to the emphasis on the manifestations in books and articles written in defense of The Toronto Blessing. Take, for example, Guy Chevreau's work, *Catch the Fire*, or Dave Roberts' journalistic account, *The Toronto Blessing*. Both books give considerable space to explaining and giving rationale for the manifestations. Many of the testimonies in Chevreau's work have the manifestations as a core element.

Likewise, on typical evenings the manifestations get a lot of attention, despite the repeated disclaimers that they are really not important. Holy Laughter sweeps the audience on given nights. When people give public testimonies, the manifestations are regularly mentioned. Some cannot even finish their testimony before another manifestation comes upon them.

After attending as often as I have, I am convinced that manifestations occupy a key place. More important, they have a dominant place in the current theology of Toronto Blessing advocates. The signs and wonders have served from the start as justification for belief in the manifest presence of God.

The Interesting Case of Mick Brown

Any analysis of the manifestations must take into acount the December 3, 1994 issue of *Telegraph* magazine, in which Mick Brown recounts his visit to the "Catch the Fire" conference in Toronto held the previous October. His article came out under the title, "Unzipper Heaven, Lord. Ha-ha, Ho-ho, He-he." Brown ends his account in a provocative way:

> I found myself beside John Arnott. . . . I didn't even see his hand coming as it arced through the air and touched me gently— hardly at all—on the forehead. . . . I could feel a palpable shock running through me, then I was falling backwards, as if my legs had been kicked away from under me.
>
> I hit the floor—I swear this is the truth—laughing like a drain.

Two things make this account important. (1) Brown does not claim to be a Christian, and so it is fascinating that Arnott's touch caused him to have the Toronto experience. (2) Brown's perspective has been used by those critical of The Toronto Blessing to argue that the force behind Arnott is obviously not the Holy Spirit, since Brown was not converted as a result of the alleged heavenly touch.

What should one make of this particular case? There can be no doubt that Brown was not radically changed by his experience in Toronto. He was interviewed in considerable detail by the British publication *Evangelicals Now*. Brown affirmed his doubts about evangelical Christianity and compares the experience he had in Toronto with something similar that occurred when he was reporting on an Indian religious leader named Mother Meera. His experience at the hand of Meera did not have any long-term consequences. "Nor did I have any long-term consequence from the 'Toronto Blessing,'" he added. "What happened was that I fell down laughing, as I described, and was on the floor for about ten minutes. I got up rather dazed but perfectly happy and relaxed." The report in *Evangelicals Now* goes on to suggest that we might be "witnessing in what the majority of cases is an essentially non-Christian experience, which some Christians are trying to assimilate into their view of the Christian life." The writer concludes with the comment: "If so, this could be a very significant turning point in the history of current evangelicalism."

The Brown case must be handled carefully. It would be rather tenuous to hinge the entire interpretation of The Toronto Blessing on one subjective experience by a reporter with New Age leanings. In fact, there is something inconsistent about the weight critics given to this one report of a non-Christian in contrast to the skepticism they feel toward the testimonies of thousands of Christians about the same reality. The defenders of The Toronto Blessing can easily answer the concerns of the authors of *Evangelicals Now* magazine, claiming that the Lord was gracious to Mick Brown by granting him an experience of his touch and power. Unfortunately, Brown did not look beyond the sign to the Sign-giver; instead, he resorted to interpreting the experience in the light of his New Age ideology and thus missed an opportunity to dedicate his life to Jesus Christ.

Decently and in Order?

Finally, the most popular objection to the manifestations is that they involve chaos in worship. This criticism is shared by MacArthur, Hanegraaff, Smith, and others. Many believe that The Toronto Blessing is in violation of the Pauline injunction about divine worship: "But everything should be done in a fitting and orderly way" (1 Cor. 14:40). That command follows Paul's earlier instruction that truly meaningful worship involves the priority of love (13:1–14:1), the necessity of intelligent communication (14:2–25), and the orderly exercise of gifts, particularly prophecy (14:26–39). On this last point, Paul writes that "God is not a God of disorder but of peace" (14:33). Gordon Fee writes about the Corinthian situation:

> Now Paul is arguing that the basis of all these instructions is ultimately theological. It has to do with the character of God, probably vis-à-vis the deities of the cults, whose worship was characterized by frenzy and disorder. The theological point is crucial: the character of one's deity is reflected in the character of one's worship.[7]

Toronto Blessing apologists have frequently tried to defend the manifestations in light of criticism about chaos and unintelligibility. We therefore ask the question: Have Airport Vineyard leaders disobeyed the Bible's command that "everything should be done in a fitting and orderly way"?

Let us first note that what amounts to order for one Christian may seem chaotic to another. That is, a Presbyterian may view a Baptist meeting as unruly, while a Baptist may consider a Pentecostal service chaotic, and the latter may view a typical night at the Airport Vineyard as out of line. In other words, this issue is an area where Christians simply disagree on what constitutes obedience to specific biblical teaching.

However, the fact that there is a continuum does not mean that the issue is simply one of private opinion. One can still pursue the question of what constitutes "fitting and orderly" worship. Vineyard leaders must not so easily sidestep legitimate questions about intelligible and meaningful worship, as if these Bible-based concerns can be dismissed by a quick reference to the work of the Spirit.

The burden of proof here lies clearly upon The Toronto Blessing apologists. All things being equal, typical evening meetings press the boundaries of what even the most generous charismatic would call "fitting and orderly." Many of the more bizarre manifestations lack meaning. Furthermore, it is obviously risky when crowds are given space to revel in religious ecstasy, some of which may have subtle sexual elements. Moreover, the "animal behavior" surely deserves severe caution. Some critics say that the Vineyard has become a "barnyard." It is no wonder that John Wimber has been hesitant about these manifestations. They have brought the Vineyard into much disrepute in many Christian churches.

Consider this account from John Arnott. He speaks about people "prophetically acting like lions and oxen and eagles and even warriors." He refers to a situation in another church, where someone was "acting like an eagle, flying around the room." The person would not stop, so it was suggested that they "throw a rabbit out in the middle of the floor," and maybe the eagle would come down.[8] Is this really "fitting and orderly"?

In the same message Arnott refers to a woman "on all fours, snorting and pawing the ground like an angry bull." What course in hermeneutics will explain this kind of behavior? And what about the meaning of all the chopping, waving, head-shaking, twitching, and other more radical body contortions that occur at the nightly meetings? It is hard enough for Christians to agree on the meaning of Scripture. Must we now spend valuable time sorting through the wilder manifestations?

These concerns often fall on deaf ears in the zeal to defend everything connected with The Toronto Blessing. Vineyard apologists have found anything in the Bible that represents something strange or unusual as rationale. Thus, the radical behavior of an Old Testament prophet or some unique action of Jesus in a particular healing miracle is used to justify the excesses in current Vineyard worship.

What is at issue here, however, is not that God may do something radical in the life of a particular prophet. No one debates this. Likewise, no one objects to Jesus' performing some healing miracle in an unusual way. These are specific and isolated incidents that have little to do with what constitutes normative and regular worship in the church. Paul's command that divine worship involves meaning and order still stands as the word of the Spirit for us today.

Given this, it seems that the Vineyard has erred in relation to the excesses that have been tolerated. Hopefully, there will be a closer monitoring of actions that are wild and out of control. The leaders ought to realize the dangers of unfettered human psyches in the setting of zealous worship. The Holy Spirit is not quenched by more faithful obedience to the instructions that he gave to a charismatic church long ago.

In recent months, I have noticed an establishment of a greater degree of serenity and order in the evening renewal meetings. I think some of the concerns about wild and bizarre actions are being addressed by the Vineyard leadership in Toronto, even if quietly behind the scenes, though this observation clashes with a word given by the Toronto prophet Marc Dupont. Recently, he said that the church has seen nothing yet and that there is going to be an even wilder sense of abandonment in worship. I would hope his prediction fails, since more extreme worship would represent further departure from the apostolic principle referred to above.

Since the manifestations are secondary, as Vineyard leaders state regularly, those Christians who do not engage in them are in no danger of quenching the Holy Spirit. Unfortunately, the manifestations have had a life of their own, though this is due in part to the focus and defense given to them by Vineyard leaders.

Of course, every excess in The Toronto Blessing is matched by dull and lifeless worship from so many corners of the Christian church. In light of this sad reality, the above cautions must be set in a final word of appreciation for the vitality and exuberance that The Toronto Blessing has brought to thousands of Christians. Ian Rennie, one of Canada's leading church historians, has said it well:

> No reading of the Book of Acts will suggest that the ministry of the Holy Spirit is always quiet and inner. In adopting such an attitude we may be cutting ourselves off from the activity of the sovereign Spirit which we all so much need, and consigning our congregations to harmonious sterility.[9]

Seven
Three Healing Cases

While The Toronto Blessing has not been described as a healing revival, frequent claims have been made for supernatural healings at Airport Vineyard meetings and in other worship settings connected with the Toronto outpouring of the Spirit.

Some preliminary judgments will situate my approach to such claims. In principle, I believe that it is possible for God to perform miracles and that he can still do them today. Rejection of the miraculous owes its chief debt to David Hume, a leader of the Enlightenment, who wrote a classic essay that allegedly proved that miracles are impossible or, at the very least, cannot be used to establish the truth of a religion.

There are at least two replies that one might make to Hume. (1) If his theories were correct, they would constitute a powerful blow against the heart of the Christian gospel. Miraculous claims stand at the center of the message and ministry of Jesus Christ. (2) There is no logical reason to accept the view that miracles are impossible. Some question whether Hume held this view or the milder one that miracles are simply hard to prove. In any case, the God who can create a universe should have no problem performing a specific miracle. If one can believe in God as Creator, why should one doubt that he can heal?

In other words, I see no valid biblical or theological reasons to argue that miracles are not for today. Many Christians believe, however, that the "age of miracles" ended with the completion of the New Testament and the end of the apostolic era. Those who advance this cessationist view often appeal to 1 Corinthians 13:9–10: "For we know in part and we prophecy in part, but when perfection comes, the imperfect disappears." They interpret this text to be saying that the gifts of the Spirit are the "imperfect [that] disappears" and that the finalized Bible represents the "perfection" that takes its place.[1]

In a slightly different version of this view, F. David Farnell argues that the gifts of tongues, prophecy, and miracles ceased after the apostolic era because they were only intended for the church in its infancy. Farnell thinks that the Greek word translated in the NIV as "perfection" is better understood as "maturity." Thus, at the end of the apostolic period, with the church firmly established, there was no further need for signs and wonders.[2]

Gordon Fee, on the other hand, has argued against the cessationist perspective in any of its forms. Writing about the disputed Corinthian passage, he argues that the apostle is not talking about a contrast between immaturity and maturity. Rather, "Paul's distinctions are between 'now' and 'then,' between what is incomplete (though perfectly appropriate to the church's present existence) and what is complete (when its final destiny in Christ has been reached and 'we see face to face' and 'know as we are known')."[3] Fee adds this powerful observation to his scholarly exegetical work: "It is perhaps an indictment of Western Christianity that we should consider 'mature' our rather totally cerebral and domesticated—but bland—brand of faith, with the concomitant absence of the Spirit in terms of his supernatural gifts!"[4]

I am inclined to agree with Fee's exegesis. For my purposes here, I second his basic attitude that the Spirit's work cannot be limited by the boundaries of the apostolic period. Therefore, claims about healing cannot be dismissed a priori or automatically.

Of course, there is a huge difference between believing that miracles can happen and claiming that one or more miracles have actually taken place. At this point, the issue becomes a matter of investigation and analysis. Miracle claims have to be examined case by case, and assessment must be made of the reliability of the reports and the integrity of observers and/or those who have allegedly been healed.

John Arnott, senior pastor at the Airport Vineyard, invited me to investigate some of the claims of miraculous healing connected with his church. I picked three of the more dramatic reports and asked two medical doctors to help me in the analysis. The reasons for my seeking their assistance was twofold. (1) My doctorate is in theology, not medicine. I had learned from previous study of medical claims of New Age therapy that I was not equipped to analyze medical issues on my own. (2) I did not want my conclusions based solely on my private analysis. The Bible speaks of matters being "established by the testimony of two or three witnesses" (Deut. 19:15; Matt. 18:16). Healing and miracle stories are too often rooted in one person's private story. Given this, it would be inappropriate to make my analysis simply a record of private study.

If time had permitted, I might have picked other miracle claims to investigate, but I based my initial choice of which reports to study on three criteria: (1) the alleged miracle had to be one widely known in the Vineyard; (2) the claim had to be clearly miraculous in nature; and (3) the miraculous claim had to be testable in some way.

The David Stark Case

At the first anniversary service of The Toronto Blessing (Jan. 20, 1995), John Arnott announced to the massive congregation that David Stark of Bellevue, Washington, had been healed of cancer at a December 15 renewal meeting. Arnott read a letter (dated Dec. 29, 1994) from Stark's physician (Dr. Kyle Bryan), which stated that David's "clinical response following the prayer meeting in Toronto is nothing short of miraculous." The Airport Vineyard newsletter reported that "doctors [had] estimated his life span in hours as cancer consumed his body."[5]

Connie Janzen, an administrative assistant to John Arnott, sent me a copy of Dr. Bryan's letter, along with a longer report of David Stark's medical history and condition. I shared these two items with Dr. John Axler, a Christian friend who has a general practice in Toronto. He agreed to help me in the medical research for this book.

Our initial reaction to the letter and report was somewhat cautious. We both noticed that the letter from Dr. Bryan made it plain that full medical testing had not been done on David between his return from Toronto and the writing of the letter. However, Dr. Bryan saw no need for MRI scanning at the time. Blood tests had shown "good function" of David's bone marrow and, according to the letter, his "overall status" had "dramatically improved." What was also clearly noticeable to Dr. Bryan was the change in David's pain level. This was also what impressed those who first heard of David's healing when he spoke at the evening rally on December 15, 1994, at the Airport Vineyard. David told the crowd that at 3:40 that afternoon, he had been touched by God and that his severe pain had been taken away.

David had told Vineyard leaders that upon his return to Bellevue, he would get medical proof of his healing. He followed through by sending a copy of Dr. Bryan's December 29 letter to Toronto, along with his medical history as written on December 12. John Arnott believed that this was sufficient evidence to be able to announce David's healing at the anniversary service.

After reading the medical report, Dr. Axler told me that he thought it was a bit premature to use the word "miraculous" in describing David's case. Though Dr. Axler was impressed by the liberation from pain that David had experienced, he did not think that was sufficient reason to use the term "miracle."

I phoned David Stark personally in early February. I wanted to talk to him directly and to get his permission for Dr. Bryan to talk with us. (Dr. Bryan had stated earlier that he would not talk about the case without David's release.) David's wife answered the phone and mentioned that they had one miracle but needed another. She then shared the sad news that MRI scanning had shown that David's cancer was growing.

I then talked briefly with David and called him back that same evening in a conference call with Dr. Axler. David shared his testimony about the December visit to Toronto and his release from pain. He said that he was going to exercise faith to believe that God would anoint him again and that the cancer would be completely eradicated. "I was healed in a miraculous way in Toronto," he stated, but he also admitted that the cancer was still there.

David went on to state that we had called him too early and that later contact would show that his case was one of healing in progress. He invited us to confirm his deliverance from pain with his pastor, Wendell Smith. That release from pain, however, was authenticated for us through the work of a television crew from the Canadian Broadcasting Corporation, who had flown to Washington to interview David for a report on *The Fifth Estate*. Their report showed clips from the Vineyard's videotape of the December meeting where David gave his testimony. Furthermore, David was interviewed on camera, along with his wife, pastor, and doctor. No one could deny that David had experienced tremendous release from pain.

What is more debatable, however, is the actual extent of the deliverance from cancer. John Arnott told the CBC that he was sad to hear about the latest medical report, but that he was praying (along with thousands of believers) that David's initial touch from God would be matched with a full cure and recovery.

Before concluding this section, I want to mention one more thing. The CBC documentary handled the healing story with sensitivity and integrity. Christians often assume the worst from the media, sometimes for good reason. But in this case, David Stark felt affirmed by the reporter and crew who visited him. The reporter also gave John Arnott a chance to respond publicly to developments in the case. The CBC could have simply juxtaposed Arnott's announcement of a cure on January 20 with the later contradictory reports. Instead, the producer felt it was only fair to inform the Airport Vineyard leadership about the latest developments in the Stark case to get a response.

Angels Heal Cases of Dyslexia

The two other cases I have chosen to examine are dealt with in Guy Chevreau's book *Catch the Fire* and are mentioned in a variety of other publications. Chevreau includes dramatic testimony about angels healing children of dyslexia. This account centers on two families in Hopkinsville, Kentucky, who claimed healing in relation to The Toronto Blessing in late February, 1994. One of the persons claimed to be healed is Heather Harvey, who was thirteen at the time. She is the daughter of Graham Harvey, the pastor of the Vineyard Church in that town.

> When she received the prayer for dyslexia, she fell to the floor very still. Later she told us that angels had done brain surgery. She heard God instructing them, and was told to be very still because "this is very delicate surgery." She also reported that one of the angels got so excited that she began playing with Heather's brain, and that God had to calm her down, saying, "This is very serious, and not the time to play." (She thought that was funny.) [6]

One initial point should be made regardless of the truth or falsity of the healing. It is hard to imagine in what sense God or his angels would find such work "delicate surgery." It is being done on the concrete floor of a church by angelic forces who obviously do not need to worry about hospital regulations. Moreover, is anything hard for God? And if it was a matter of such delicacy, why would one angel be playing around with her brain? One would expect some discipline for such "unangelic" behavior.

Am I just being a hardhearted skeptic? No, I truly hope that Heather has been healed by angels at the Airport Vineyard. If included in the healing is a little angelic mischief, well, that would be worth the price. But readers should note the contradictions raised in the report itself.

Heather returned with her family to Kentucky. She went immediately to pray for her friend Monica Morgan-Dohner, who also had dyslexia. Monica told her mother what happened after Heather's prayer. "The angels shaved my head, across the top of it, from ear to ear. Then they cut my head, pulled the front of it open, and took out my brain." Monica told her mother what part of the brain needed surgery. After the angels put her brain back in her head, Monica said she "could feel the tug of stitches, across the top of my head." After this angelic surgery,

> Heather, Monica, and Monica's sister, Autumn Morgan-Dohner, began praying for anyone who had dyslexia. Heather and Autumn both have been able to watch the angels' movements during what they all refer to as "brain surgery." The adults have stood by, and watched, but stayed out of their way.[7]

I contacted Graham Harvey by phone in January of 1995, and he was responsive to my inquiry. He admitted that the focus on angels had been a bit unnerving, saying: "I believe God has done something and the focus should be on him, not on angels." He also told me that his daughter has some "emotional issues" to deal with in relation to her longtime condition. Furthermore, he said that neither Heather or Monica have been tested medically since the healings a year earlier, though he has "no doubt" that they saw angels and that the term "miracle" is appropriate to describe their healing. He has seen such a remarkable difference in them that he believes it is a matter of divine intervention.

Since I have had little experience with dyslexia and am not a medical doctor, I asked Dr. Sharon Cohen for her assistance and comments on these healing reports. She is assistant professor in the Department of Medicine and in the Graduate Department of Speech Pathology at the University of Toronto. She also informed me that psychological attitude can explain significant improvement in reading patterns, although there is no human cure for dyslexia. Only medical tests would show absolutely whether these two girls have been healed.

In light of this medical expert's opinion, I faxed Graham Harvey a letter, dated February 28, 1995, and asked him for further update. I also asked him to consider this request: "Would your church be willing to get the doctor who has diagnosed Heather and Monica in the past to do medical testing to confirm the healing?" I told him what I had heard from Dr. Cohen. I also stated:

My request is rather bold and I understand any hesitancy you might have in this regard. However, it would be wonderful if [these cases] could be confirmed by professionals who know what to look for in examining whether or not the dyslexia is gone. I hope you can accept this request in the spirit it is given, that is, I do believe that God can and does perform miracles. ... Nevertheless, in the investigation of specific claims, it certainly helps to have (support) by medical analysis and testing.

By early April, 1995, I had not heard back from Graham Harvey, and I was becoming concerned that my request may have offended him. On April 5, I sent a follow-up fax, including a copy of my earlier letter. Immediately I got a fax back from him, indicating that follow-up material would arrive shortly. On April 13, Graham sent me an update on his daughter's case plus a copy of a longer report from Melanie Morgan-Dohner concerning her daughter Monica. The two reports are given below in somewhat abbreviated form. Graham wrote:

> Concerning the healings of dyslexia in Heather Harvey's and Monica Morgan-Dohner's lives one year later, there is much rejoicing here. We cannot afford to pay the fees for testing. We are rejoicing because of Heather's progress in her schooling. She has been able to increase three years in her math work! This time last year she was in the fourth grade level of language arts. Now she is starting the seventh grade level. She no longer experiences the letter or word confusion she had before her healing.
>
> She used to hate reading, because of all the tricks the words and letters would play in her mind. She would get extremely frustrated. Now she reads three books (averaging over 100 pages each) a week. She loves reading!
>
> I asked Heather how she would summarize the difference. She said, "I can understand everything I read and work on, and enjoy doing it now." I asked my mother, who we call "Oma," the same thing. Oma said, "Heather is always reading a book now instead of watching TV, which is a big difference for her. She talks positive about school and you know she is enjoying it. Also, there has been a big difference in Heather's attitude towards her-

self—she is much more self-confident and at peace with herself."
Our lives are different! There has been a definite change in my
daughter's life.

Graham's letter continues with another account of healing from
dyslexia, a ten-year-old girl prayed for by the youth at the Hopkinsville Vineyard. He then gives a testimony about it from the girl's
mother.

> The thing she was most excited about was the six math word
> problems her daughter had to do when they returned. The mother
> stressed to me how her daughter had never, ever been able to
> think abstractly, so math word problems might as well have been
> in Hebrew. Her daughter read the problems, worked them, and
> came up with the wrong answer. So Mom asks for an explanation.
> The daughter explains all six problems, chooses the right numbers
> to work with, but just makes a math error in figuring the answer.
> The mom was so excited because this was the first time her
> daughter had ever understood a math word problem!

Graham said he would be sending me a copy of updated WISC-R
I.Q. tests that were done on this girl, whose identity is being kept
secret so that she will not be hurt by the earlier low test results.

Melanie Morgan-Dohner and her husband work as psychother-
apists at the Hopkinsville Vineyard. Here is an abbreviated report of
Melanie's update on their daughter Monica.

> It has been a year since Heather Harvey prayed for her and
> she experienced healing. In that year, her life has changed dra-
> matically. I do not know if this will help you with your article, as
> we have not had Monica tested by a doctor, but I want you to
> know more. Over the years Monica was tested many times, in
> order to get her special help in school. The testing always verified
> her limitations, and I was always grateful for the help that came
> after testing. In the past year, we have come to believe that she
> was healed of the learning disability that she had struggled with
> since her first years in school.
>
> Perhaps you do not understand fully what it is to have a
> dyslexic person in the family. It is not that person's struggle

alone. Since Monica was four years old (she is now twelve), this has been something shared by the family. As a family, we have worked with her, been frustrated at her and with her, and cried with her. We had come to know that instructions would always have to be explained slowly, that signs would have to be read out loud, that menus would have to be interpreted, that subtitles on a movie screen would have to be whispered, and that homework would require hours and hours every day. There was never a day that we weren't all being touched by her inability to process symbols, letters, and numbers.

For Monica, of course, it was the hardest. She is the one who had to cope with the feelings of inadequacy, of not being able to keep up with her friends, and of not being able to understand. She learned that she could count on us to be at the school, every year, making sure that Monica was getting extra help and that her teachers understood her limitations.

When Heather told Monica that she was going to pray for her dyslexia to be healed, she did not tell Monica the story of her experience. Monica had not heard it from anyone. When she got up off the floor, she told a story remarkably similar to Heather's. The first thing that she said was, "I feel like I have all the pieces to my puzzle for the first time." Then she talked about seeing angels and feeling work being done in her head. Did we have some theology for this, and did it all make complete sense to us? Not at all. Not in the least. We didn't know what to expect.

For the next week, Monica reported each day, "I understood what was going on at school today!" She was quite amazed by it. What was I doing? Praying, "Please God, let it be real." As the days went by, she changed so dramatically that we couldn't not see it. She was interested in her homework and eager to do it. She picked out some books that she wanted to read. These were books she had seen her friends read, that we had not been able to get her interested in, previously. She was more than interested in them—she was using them to learn how to read. The letters in each word stayed in correct order for her. She could sound the word out, starting with the first letter. She couldn't do that before, as she normally saw the middle or ending letters as the first. For instance, she would have looked at the word "ship," and said the first sound was a "p." She has sensed before that she couldn't trust her eyes, and now she could. She had the freedom of a bird whose broken wing was finally mended.

Math had been a terribly difficult subject for Monica. She couldn't line up the figures properly, and with numbers scattered all over the page, calculations (even done on fingers) were never correct. The first week after that prayer, she brought home a paper that I refer to as "Junior Accountant." It was rows and rows of perfectly shaped, perfectly spaced numbers. I knew that no mere change in her thinking, or in her beliefs about herself, could have done that. I understand that you have been told that dyslexia doesn't "get healed" except by a miracle. That is exactly the point we are trying to make. I don't believe it gets healed except by a miracle either. I lived with it too long. I fought it with everything that I had.

At the time of her healing, Monica had been working with a home tutor. Her tutor was an experienced teacher, finishing her Master's degree in learning disabilities. She had recently done testing on Monica to verify the dyslexia. That woman was able quickly to see the difference in Monica's ability to see letters in order, in being able to accurately sound out the syllables in order, and in being able to go from one line to the next correctly.

It is very difficult to watch your child struggle and to see her not be able to grasp a thing no matter how many times it is presented. Monica was always willing to try, but never able to hold onto whatever small successes she had. If, after long periods of reading and practicing a few words she could understand them and identify them, it did not mean that she would be able to the next day. Things gained were often gone the next day. This is not happening now. She is learning and retaining. She carries a book in the car. She is discovering the joy of written stories. She is feeling successful in school, and her grades affirm that. Nothing can take this away from her, and her life will be significantly different because of it. Parts of life that were closed to her are now open.

As monumental and wondrous as her reading is to me, Monica receives this healing as just one part of knowing that God touched her. She felt his touch, and at the same time that her brain

was healed, her heart was changed forever by the knowledge that
he knows her, loves her, and wants to see her free. At twelve years
of age, she is filled with confidence in the living God. She knows
him as a God who wants to help his children, is willing and able
to heal them, and will use her to do it. She feels confidence in
asking him to heal someone else. Here is fruit that cannot be medically tested. If my child had been blind and could now see, no
one would doubt whether I could accurately tell the difference.
You can believe that it is very important to me to know what is
going on with her, and I cannot be shaken from knowing, beyond
doubt, that a miracle has happened.

These reports are exciting. Only a coldhearted soul would
ignore the wonderful release that has come to these two families.
Even the absence of medical tests is understandable. If both families know that miracles have taken place, then who cares about a
doctor's opinion? It would be like Lazarus feeling the need for medical certification of his being raised from the dead. What if the
improvement was really largely psychological and did not involve
angelic surgery, and what if the girls technically still have dyslexia?
If testing confirmed this, such a blow to the girls' sincere belief in
the divine surgery could cause them to regress in their learning disabilities. This would be tragic.

But let's assume that the two families know that this has been
a case of complete miraculous deliverance. They are convinced of
the healings and know that the best medical testing will only confirm their view. Such examination is expensive, and they probably
cannot afford it. A strong case could be made that the Airport Vineyard should consider providing documented medical proof if this
case continues to be cited as evidence of God's supernatural healing.

In response to this further material, Dr. Sharon Cohen said they
were "moving" reports. Concerning the documentation about Monica, Dr. Cohen states: "It is an impressive account of change that I
have never seen happen in an individual with such severe learning
disabilities." She also said that the fact that Heather and Monica
now have a love for reading makes their cases unique. When I asked
her if she would call these two cases miraculous, she replied that

she would only use this term if medical tests showed the absence of dyslexia. She said that she never bases her medical scientific verdict solely on the testimony of patients and their families. When I pressed her how she would bet if she had to speculate, based on the reports available, she said, "I don't bet." But she went on to say she would be willing to test the two children if they came to Toronto.

What should one think of the two accounts? Do they prove that miracles have taken place? It depends on what proof is required. Some readers will take these reports at face value and believe them without even blinking. Others will remain skeptical until medical confirmation has been obtained. And there may be some who will never believe, even if a doctor's verdict was available.

I asked one of my students who has dyslexia to read the two letters and give me her reaction. She hopes, as anyone would, that the accounts involve real miracles and that the dyslexia is gone. She also said that she has seen enough improvement in her own condition simply because of psychological attitude that she thought only medical testing can prove these particular cases beyond any doubt.

The Case of Sarah Lilliman

Chevreau's book *Catch the Fire* also mentions the fascinating story of Sarah Lilliman. This is probably the most famous healing story connected with The Toronto Blessing. It was first circulated in a Vineyard report in the spring of 1994 and has been recounted in full in Chevreau's work. It has also been related in briefer form in other places, including Dave Roberts' book.

Because the case is complicated, I will give virtually the whole account, leaving out only the last few sentences.[8]

> In October of 1991, 13-year-old Sarah caught what her parents thought was the flu. No sniffles and sneezes, however, could cause her eyesight, very poor from birth, to degenerate further; nor could the flu cause memory loss and cognitive dysfunction. Testing was done at Peel Memorial and Sick Children's Hospital, Toronto, but no medical causes for her symptoms were found. As months passed, Sarah lost more and more muscle control, as well as cognitive ability. By October, 1993, she was unable to walk,

eat, swallow, or see. In January, 1994, she was transferred to Bloorview, a hospital for chronic care patients, as she needed the aid of a mini-hoist to be put to bed.

On 27 February, 1994, Sarah's friend, Rachel Allalouf, came to the evening service at the Airport Vineyard. After Randy Clark's message, she received prayer, and while resting in the Lord, she had a vision of being at a table in heaven; her two grandfathers were there, as was Jesus. That vision "faded" to one of the cross, where Jesus told Rachel to go to Bloorview Hospital the next day and pray for Sarah. Rachel reported that Jesus told her how to pray.

The next day, Rachel went to the hospital as instructed, along with her father, Simon. Sarah was in her special wheelchair— described as a "stretcher on wheels." She recognized the voices, but could not see or comprehend what was being said to her. Saliva was dribbling out of her mouth.

Rachel and Simon moved Sarah to a quiet place in the ward, where Rachel began praying the way Jesus had told her to. As she and her father interceded over the course of the next two and a half hours, Sarah began to cry, and then shake. Her sight began to come back, and her legs started to move. She slowly began to sit up on her own, and the previously uncontrollable drooling stopped. The joy of the Lord started to fill her, and Sarah was able to say, "I'm getting stronger!"

Before coming to the hospital, Rachel was so convinced Jesus was going to heal Sarah, she had brought her friend a bag of dill pickle chips for her to eat. Over the next few days, Sarah began walking and eating on her own, even the chips! Her sight continued to improve.

Word of Sarah's recovery quickly went around the hospital. A few days later, a woman at the front desk came up to Simon and Rachel and said, "The power of Jesus is real, isn't it?" She was a believer, and as Simon reports it, "was thrilled that the Lord had come and visited the hospital with His healing power." She then asked them to pray for her alcoholic and unbelieving husband, which they did.

On 22 April, 1994, Sarah returned home from Bloorview— no one had any expectation that she would ever leave the chronic care hospital. On Tuesday, 26 April, Sarah was at the Airport meeting. Her friend Rachel was with her, and had received a further word from the Lord that if Sarah would go to the front of the church and testify, He would heal her eyes. Sarah's mother noted how hard this was for Sarah, given her terrible fear of people—"but she did it because she trusted God."

One of the prayer teams came forward, blessed Rachel, and then said to Sarah, "Tonight you will have two healings from God—He will heal your eyes and He will heal your emotions."

Sarah has since received further outpourings of the Holy Spirit, such that she is able to pray in tongues. Her whole family has undergone radical change, is now closer than ever, and has a much closer walk with God.

When I interviewed Guy Chevreau for an article in *Christianity Today*, I asked him about his own investigation of this case. He said that he had basically included this account in good faith, believing that it was an accurate summary of Sarah's case. He also said that he would be glad if I examined the case in detail.

I got the Lilliman home phone number from Connie Janzen at the Airport Vineyard, hoping that Sarah and her family would be open to contact from me. To my delight, Sarah and her parents (David and Prim) were receptive to my study of her case. I told them that I was honored by their trust, and they respected my right to reach my own conclusions.

In my first talk with the family, it was immediately clear that there were problems with both major and minor aspects of Guy's account. When I talked with Sarah, she made it plain that the healing was not as quick or as dramatic as presented in the book. And Prim told me that Sarah is still "legally blind" and that the second part of the healing story is inaccurate. When Sarah went to the Airport Vineyard on April 26, she did not receive "two healings from God—He will heal your eyes and He will heal your emotions."

Prim also questioned the view that God would heal Sarah only if she went to the front of the church to speak. Prim felt that God would not operate that way, especially given her daughter's fear in crowds and the fact that she is still mentally challenged. Whatever one concludes, Sarah and Prim's own testimony brings into suspect the accuracy of Rachel's second "word from the Lord."

With the family's full permission, Dr. John Axler and I were able to examine Sarah's medical records at the Bloorview Hospital. We spent more than two hours going through all of the reports on her case, and the Health Records department made a photocopy of some of them for our further study.[9] Based on this investigation, there are some significant difficulties with the report in *Catch the Fire*, in addition to the problems noted earlier. Some of these involve faulty impressions or mistaken assumptions, and there are also some simple mistakes in fact.

Faulty Impressions

(1) The account suggests that Sarah's medical problems began in 1991 and lasted until her healing in 1994. The problems that led to her hospitalization in 1991 actually began two years earlier, according to the medical reports. Also, these problems from which she was "healed" in 1994 had gone away after a four-week stay at the Sick Children's Hospital in 1991.

(2) In saying that "no medical causes for her symptoms were found," one could easily infer that the doctors who treated her were at a total loss and that, therefore, her improvement depended on a miracle from God. However, the medical reports make it clear that doctors thought that many of her problems were psychological in origin.

(3) The report that "by October 1993, she was unable to walk, eat, swallow or see" could be interpreted to mean that she showed no improvement in these four areas until her divine healing. Actually, during November, while she was a patient at the Sick Children's Hospital, she showed improvement in both eating and swallowing.

Mistakes in Fact

(1) Sarah was admitted to the Bloorview Hospital on December 2, 1993, not in January of 1994.

(2) When Rachel and her father Simon visited Sarah (on February 28, 1994), it is said that "she recognized voices, but could not see or comprehend what was being said to her." This may be Simon and Rachel's interpretation of Sarah's reaction to her. However, the hospital records make it clear that from December through February, Sarah could see at least partially and had regular conversations (of varying degrees) with her family and with hospital staff. To give one example, a report from a medical consultation that took place on February 21 has Sarah's response to specific and important issues.

(3) The statement that "no one had any expectation that she would ever leave the chronic care hospital" is simply false. Her medical history from 1989 through 1993 showed a pattern of decline and improvement. The medical reports also clearly suggest the possibility of recovery, given the explanation of a psychosomatic origin for some of her physical problems.

Conclusion

There is no doubt that the visit of Simon and Rachel with Sarah was the beginning of a dramatic turn in her recovery. The changes are significant enough that one might want to use the word "miracle." However, the word can only be legitimately used in Sarah's case if one restricts it to the same category as "wonderful," "thrilling," or "remarkable."

It is more accurate to describe Sarah's recovery as a dramatic psychological and physical response to prayer, friendship, and love. This love came not only from Simon and Rachel, but also from her family and from the staff at Bloorview, who were providing her with a caring environment to address some of the inner pain and anxiety that had such a crippling physical impact on her.

Some readers may find this interpretation unsettling. Does it sound too much like the "liberal" revision of some miracle stories in the Bible—for example, William Barclay's suggestion that Jesus did not walk on the water, but beside the water; or that the miracle of the feeding of the five thousand simply involved people sharing the lunches they had hidden away in their cloaks? For the record, I find such liberal views unfaithful to the biblical text. In my analysis of Sarah's case, the issue is not about belief in the supernatural power of God. Rather, it is about finding the best explanation for the actual facts of the alleged healing. In her case, I have no trouble saying that God ministered to her—not through supernatural intervention, but through dramatic forces often overlooked and undervalued: the power of prayer, Christian friendship, and human love.

Summary Observations

I realize that if this chapter offered a study of more than three cases, there might be a different conclusion to my study of healing reports. However, even these three cases justify the following observations.

(1) There is a price to pay when Vineyard leaders announce healings before they are verified over time by careful medical testing. The Stark and Lilliman cases illustrate the dangers of hasty and premature judgments.

(2) Vineyard leaders should show their commitment to truthtelling by correcting false impressions and mistaken facts concerning healing claims. In this regard, future editions of Guy Chevreau's work, *Catch the Fire*, and Dave Roberts' book, *The Toronto Blessing*, should be changed to correct the faulty reporting on the Lilliman case.

(3) The Hopkinsville case illustrates the need for charismatic groups to be willing to pay for medical specialists to confirm what appear to be wonderful and miraculous reports. When medical study is necessary in order to know precisely what has taken place, the burden for providing that support is on those who make the claim.

Eight
The Kansas City Prophets

Many have claimed that the 1994 Toronto Blessing associated with the Airport Vineyard Church had been predicted at various times during the last forty years by different modern-day prophets or recipients of a prophetic word from God. This is a significant claim, for a good number of Christian churches are not open to the gift of prophecy, and even some charismatics have strong reservations about this gift.

The next chapter will deal explicitly with prophecy as it relates to Toronto. However, one cannot understand the modern prophetic movement of the 1990s without some scrutiny of the controversy that erupted in 1990 over the Kansas City prophets.

It is not often that one charismatic pastor delivers a two-hundred-page attack against a fellow charismatic preacher. That, however, is exactly what happened in 1990 in Kansas City, when Ernie Gruen, pastor of a large Pentecostal church in Kansas, issued a lengthy document against the teachings and practices of the Kansas City Fellowship, pastored by Mike Bickle. Gruen strongly believed a "word of warning" was needed. His report, released in May of 1990, followed a January sermon in which he had criticized KCF. Both the sermon and the report created a fierce storm in the charismatic and Pentecostal world.

In the spring and summer of 1990 the Kansas City Fellowship became part of the Association of Vineyard Churches. Thereupon

John Wimber took it upon himself to mediate the dispute between Mike Bickle and Ernie Gruen, and a measure of peace was restored. Gruen agreed to stop circulation of his report, and Mike Bickle was brought under public discipline by John Wimber.

But why does this controversy need to be explored? (1) There are close links between the Kansas City prophets and The Toronto Blessing that require us to understand the prophetic ministry out of Kansas City. (2) We can learn several important principles from the way in which the prophetic element was handled in Kansas. (3) Some significant and widespread distortions should be corrected for the sake of the larger Christian community.

The Critique of Kansas City Fellowship

In his written document, Ernie Gruen expressed appreciation for the ministry of Mike Bickle, but he also stressed rising concern over developments in his church, the Kansas City Fellowship. He warned about the rise of "a charismatic heresy" and the harm that could be caused by such error.

In his report, Gruen did apologize for three errors he made in the January sermon, but he affirmed the substance of his earlier strong attack on KCF. The written document raised legitimate questions about ethical compromises, theological and prophetic teaching, and cultlike tendencies in KCF.

In 1991 I traveled to Kansas City to attend the annual meetings of the Evangelical Theological Society and the American Academy of Religion. While there I interviewed Ernie Gruen and John Arnold, the man who had done much of the research that provided the background for Gruen's allegations. With several colleagues, I also attended an evening service at the Metro Vineyard to hear Mike Bickle preach. We were each impressed with his powerful, passionate preaching.

After the Sunday evening service Mike and I went out to a nearby restaurant so that we could process some of the debate still going on over KCF and its famous prophets: John Paul Jackson, Bob Jones, and Paul Cain. We ended up talking for five hours! I spent a similar amount of time in conversation with John Arnold over the six days that I was attending the two conferences.

What, then, were Ernie Gruen's concerns? To begin, the eschatological teaching of Bob Jones deserved suspicion. Jones spoke about a new breed of "elect seed" (humans) created by God in 1973 to form a super-church that would be ten thousand times greater than the church of the book of Acts. Furthermore, Jones and Paul Cain were teaching that Kansas City was going to be headquarters for a group of super-Christians who would form "Joel's Army" and prepare for the final end-time harvest of souls to herald the return of Jesus Christ.

Gruen was also rightly alarmed about the elitism that dominated much of the teaching in KCF. Jones and Cain in particular were elevated to a high prophetic status. Perhaps unintentionally, Mike Bickle was beginning to picture his group of churches as the center of God's work in America.

The document from Gruen also noted how some of the theology of KCF was rooted in the private, mystical experiences of Bob Jones. His miraculous journeys to heaven and hell amounted to subjective testimony and did not deserve the attention they received— especially given Bob Jones's inability to prophesy accurately about earthly things and the *prima facie* extremism of his claims.

Consider this dialogue between Mike Bickle and Bob Jones as one example of a wild claim.

MB: "Wait, wait, the Lord just said who would you like to see?"

BJ: "Yeah, and I said, 'The Apostle Paul,' and He said, 'There he is.' And I looked at this man and I said, 'That's not Paul!' 'Yes, that is Paul.' 'That's Paul?' 'Yeah.' Uh, little bitty man with an oversized bald head, and his head was sort of cocked on the side and he's sort of stooped shoulders and I looked at him and I could see that this body had really suffered, and I said, 'Lord, You mean that this man endured all that I read?' He said, 'Yeah.' 'But he looks sort of deformed.' 'He really is a little bit thataway because of all the sufferin' that he went through.'"

MB: "Bob, one thing that I want you to add to that. That's the accountability factor. But there's another factor—that Paul was anxious—'cause he said that he [Bob Jones] came running up to him and said, 'You're Paul.' And he [Paul] said, 'But you're a prophet from the end-time generation; you've far surpassed your generation, mine.' And he says, 'And I have a right to hear you first.' Because Paul was anxious to talk to the end-time apostles and prophets more than the end-time apostles and prophets would've been to talk to Paul. He said, 'Because what they would do would go far greater in the glory of God.''

The teachings and prophecies of Bob Jones and John Paul Jackson were sometimes false and often foolish, and Gruen rightly warned about these characteristics. For example, Jackson said in one message that God blew up the space shuttle Challenger to teach Americans a lesson, given that there was a teacher on board. And Bob Jones predicted that one thousand religious leaders would be killed by God in 1990.

But there were also weaknesses in Gruen's report. He could have spent more time outlining the positive side of KCF and the biblical nature of much of its ministry. Standing alone, the document did not do justice to the depth and breadth of Bickle's preaching. Furthermore, I think the report too quickly attributed "occult" power to Bob Jones and resorted too readily to overt connections with the satanic.

Using the principle of Occam's razor (that one should generally accept the least complex explanation), it is perhaps judicious to conclude that Bob Jones was careless with facts, mistaken in his prophetic speculations, and overcome by his visionary, mystical experiences. Likewise, Bickle allowed his high-powered vision to be clouded and derailed by gullibility over the prophetic phenomenon.

The Vineyard Response to Gruen

John Wimber's personal involvement in the whole controversy was exemplary. His work with Mike Bickle and Bob Jones in 1990 was redemptive, and his correspondence and face-to-face contact with Ernie Gruen was likewise open, positive, and healing.

Unfortunately, these earlier accomplishments were marred by the release of an unbalanced and faulty reply to Gruen published in the Vineyard magazine, *Equipping the Saints*. The article, under Wimber's signature, was basically from Jack Deere's report on the crisis. (1) It announced the ridiculous wholesale verdict that "Pastor Gruen's accusations are untrue." (2) It gave undue emphasis to Gruen's admitted errors in his January sermons and overstated Gruen's weaknesses. (3) It offered a pathetic defense against some of Gruen's accusations. (4) It failed to give sufficient acknowledgment of the wild claims, foolish prophecies, false predictions, and emerging elitist spirit evident in the material documented by Gruen. (5) Finally, it failed to note the distinction between a plausible interpretation of the Bible's prophetic passages and an eschatology far removed from exegesis and rooted instead in the subjective, mystical experiences of Bob Jones, John Paul Jackson, and Paul Cain.

An implicit contradiction in the way that both KCF and the Vineyard described the prophets in their midst also developed. Under criticism, Bob Jones and the other visionaries were not described as "prophets." Reference was made only to a prophetic office or to the occasional exercise of "prophecy" in certain individuals. In Mike Bickle's sermons and in David Pytches' book, *Some Said It Thundered*, however, the accent was on the arrival of a "new breed of prophets."

I had read about the whole debate and the Vineyard reply to Gruen *before* actually getting Gruen's two-hundred page report. Given the scathing review of Gruen in *Equipping the Saints*, I expected to find his report shallow and rooted in biased testimony. I expected quotations to be taken out of context or evidence twisted to make a case. However, my comparison of Gruen's charges with sermons from KCF made it plain to me that Gruen had every right to warn the charismatic world.

When the Vineyard report against Gruen was released, the Kansas City pastor decided that the Lord did not want him to reply.

He hoped that Bickle would learn from his discipline under Wimber and that things would improve in Bickle's churches. In fact, Wimber did bring significant order and correction to Bickle's work and to the prophetic ministries of Bob Jones and John Paul Jackson.

When I interviewed John Wimber in September of 1991, he said that the prophets would not be loose cannons on the Vineyard ship. They would be bolted down to the deck, or they would be told to exercise their gifts elsewhere. He spoke in no uncertain terms about the need for discipline in the gift of prophecy. Though the Vineyard leadership never publicly apologized to Ernie Gruen for their highly skewed reply, John Wimber did contact him privately to express his regret that their response to him was so careless and unbalanced.

David Pytches' Analysis of Kansas City

David Pytches, the well-known Anglican renewal leader, gave a "rosy" and overly optimistic interpretation of KCF in his international best-seller, *Some Said It Thundered*.[1] Unfortunately, his account is not the place to turn for judicious and balanced investigation. In an article I wrote in *The Canadian Baptist* (March-April, 1992), I stated that the second edition of Pytches' work is marred by an "intemperate" foreward by John White. Dr. White, in a spirit of graciousness, wrote me later and agreed that my verdict was correct. My view was based on his harsh statements about Ernie Gruen and his uncritical acceptance of the Vineyard's written reply about Gruen.

The main body of Pytches' work fails on several levels. For one thing, it uncritically adopts the views of Mike Bickle, Bob Jones, and Paul Cain. The most amazing claims are accepted without historical analysis or without critical reflection in the spirit of the Bible's command to "test all things." For example, the book begins with a prophecy (given in August, 1989) by Bob Jones to astronaut James Irwin that gave the location of Noah's ark, and the book concludes by citing speculation that the ark had been found. In fact, however, the ark had not been found even by the time of the revised edition of the book, but this fact gets no mention. This does not mean that Jones, Cain, and Bickle get the story of KCF confused or that every prophecy is inaccurate. What needs emphasis here is Pytches' methodological weakness in approaching claims that are stupendous without examining them. They deserve more analysis before any endorsement.

Pytches also gave insufficient weight to the pervasiveness of private, subjective "miracles" in the life of Bob Jones in particular (also true to some extent of Paul Cain). Bob Jones is particularly adept at private visions or private trips to heaven. His teaching about end-time prophecy or the demonic is rooted in what he was allegedly told in his private encounters with God and the demonic world. One longs for the example of Jesus, who confirmed his authority from heaven by stupendous miracles that were in the public domain. Naturally, one cannot expect that every event in the life of an alleged prophet be accessible to the crowds. Nevertheless, too much emphasis in KCF history was given to subjective and tenuous realities.

In addition, Pytches glossed over the tough questions that must be asked about KCF or other aspects of charismatic Christianity. For example, he refers to David Harrell's famous historical work on the healing revivals of the 1940s and 1950s. What Pytches does not seem to know is that Harrell is skeptical about the miraculous claims of the famous revivalists of the day.

Pytches' claim that the KCF leaders were "humble" also seems paradoxical in light of their self-exaltation as leaders of "Joel's Army" and as the "new breed" of Christians who will not give into the temptations of glory, gold, and girls. This kind of bravado seems not only a signal of pride but of an underlying lack of self-confidence.

Moreover, Pytches' history about the early days of KCF only gave the positive side. He did not make any contact with sensitive Christians who were part of that early fellowship and who felt that the arrival of Bob Jones harmed the powerful, biblical vision of Mike Bickle.

As another criticism, Pytches gave insufficient attention to the fact that many of Bob Jones's predictions were announced *ex post facto*. People were informed by Jones himself about his phenomenal prophecies from God, but only after the events occurred. This is a troublesome habit in modern-day prophets.[2]

Prophetic Power in Kansas City?

People have offered four explanations for the ministry of Bob Jones, Paul Cain, and the other prophets connected with Kansas City. (1) Some argue that there have been no supernatural healings, prophecies, or words of knowledge connected with any of these men. (2) Others contend that the prophecies and miracles are demonic in origin. I have seen one prophecy chart that includes the Vineyard and KCF as part of the tangled web of the Antichrist in the formation of the One World Church. (3) Some Christians believe that the prophetic gifting in KCF was real but often abused, authentic but often careless. These prophets carry the treasure in earthen vessels like all Christians and therefore sometimes fail in the exercise of their gifts. In this vein, some Vineyard leaders believe that Bob Jones and Paul Cain are not remarkable in prophetic ability but are sometimes amazing in words of knowledge. (4) Jack Deere has been a strong advocate of the view that Paul Cain is radically different from Bob Jones or any other modern-day prophet. He contends that Cain is basically totally accurate in both prophecy and word of knowledge.

In my judgment, the third option is the best one. After considerable investigation, I am convinced that God has given specific, accurate, and dramatic words of knowledge to both Jones and Cain. However, some caveats are in order. I remain almost totally skeptical of the alleged prophetic messages given to Bob Jones. Also, contrary to Jack Deere, I believe that Paul Cain has made significant errors in both prophecy and words of knowledge. For example, he has said that John Wimber was to be "the End-Time Apostle" to lead Joel's Army and that Wimber was "unique in all the earth." To his credit, John Wimber has refused this kind of prophetic speculation.

The reason I am willing to credit both Cain and Jones with some gifting in "word of knowledge" is because of the specific and clear examples of accurate discernment that I have heard from many fine and trustworthy Christians. I cannot believe that these examples are all simply wish fulfillment or lies or distortions. In one case, for example, Paul Cain received a word from God to give encouragement to a Christian leader about unresolved sin. The sin that plagued this leader was known only to him. This person asked God to give Cain a word of assurance about this particular burden. When Cain met with him, he accurately identified the sin and assured the person that this was forgiven by his heavenly Father.

The Unique Case of Paul Cain

Anyone remotely familiar with prophetic ministry knows of the enormous influence that Paul Cain has had on John Wimber and the Vineyard movement. In fact, it would be impossible to understand the last eight years of the Vineyard movement without some knowledge of the ministry of Paul Cain. There are several reasons he should be viewed as a unique case in the study of the Kansas City prophets and the Vineyard.

(1) Cain's status as a biblical seer survived virtually unscathed in the aftermath of the battle over the Kansas City prophets. Wimber brought no discipline to him, but instead focused on Mike Bickle, Bob Jones, and John Paul Jackson. Gruen even backed down from the serious allegations he had raised against Cain in a brief section of his report.[3] For example, Cain's claim, denied by Gruen, that he had worked with William Branham, a controversial healing revivalist of an earlier generation, proved to be accurate.

(2) Cain's role as a healer and evangelist in the late 1940s and 1950s also justifies the distinction between himself and the other KCF prophets. A brief biographical account of Cain states that "although he was a Baptist he found himself drafted into the healing movement which swept through America. He became one of the most prominent names in this movement."[4]

(3) From 1988 through 1991, there was no doubt that Cain had "superstar" status in the Vineyard. Conferences were held worldwide with Cain as the featured speaker. The Vineyard magazine even went so far as to refer to him as "a new breed of man."[5] That serious bit of elitist rhetoric is just one indication of how highly the Vineyard regarded Cain.

In early 1992 I was able to speak by phone with Cain after he taught at a large conference at the Anaheim Vineyard. He agreed to respond by fax to several crucial questions. Here is a copy of my queries to Cain and his replies.

JB: Would you call yourself a prophet, and if so, in what sense?

PC: "I do not call myself a prophet. If the Lord wants me to have that title, then the Lord will have to establish that."

JB: Are there any major errors in prophetic word or in your dealings with people that you have made in your work with Kansas City Fellowship and the Vineyard?

PC: "By no means am I an infallible person, nor do I claim to have an infallible ministry. However, at this present time I am not aware of any major errors in my ministry with Kansas City Fellowship or the Vineyard. I am not saying that I haven't made major errors. I am saying that I'm not aware of any major errors in my relationship with these ministries."

JB: What did the Lord say to you that helped the Vineyard through a crisis in the summer of 1988? How did your word help stop a conspiracy or a wrong direction in the Vineyard?

PC: "This is not for public information. This is family business within the Vineyard, which neither I nor the Vineyard have any intention of making public."

JB: What would you say is your major burden or message for the Vineyard today, as well as for the greater evangelical world?

PC: "Regarding the Vineyard specifically, I believe God has raised it up to speak to that part of the church which has rejected the supernatural gifts of the Holy Spirit. I want to see the Vineyard fulfill this calling and come into 'the measure of the stature of the fullness of Christ' that Ephesians 4:13 promises. I want to see the greater evangelical world return to full confidence in the power of the blood of Christ. The gospel teaches us that there is power in the blood of Christ not only to forgive us, but to change us. It seems to me that much of the church has lost their confidence in the power of the blood of Christ to change us. I want to see a church that knows both the Scriptures and the unlimited power of the blood of Jesus Christ."

How should we interpret and respond to Paul Cain's ministry, the claims the Vineyard had made about him, and his own self-understanding? I think a balanced and accurate response involves the following assertions.

(1) Most everyone who meets Paul Cain experiences him to be a gentle man. I met him at a prophecy conference in Hamilton, Ontario, in 1993 and found him to be delightful and warm. Kenn Gulliksen, the founder of the Vineyard movement, told me one time that what most impressed him about Cain was not his prophetic ability (which Kenn strongly affirmed), but his love and care.

(2) I have no problem affirming that Cain is orthodox in his basic theology, something we might credit to his strong Baptist roots in the state of Texas. He was born in Garland (near Dallas) in 1929 and was tutored in his early years by the pastor of Garland's First Baptist Church. Cain's later association with and current commendation of William Branham (who died in 1965) has led some to dismiss Cain completely. What should be noted here is that Cain had little long-term contact with Branham. Moreover, Branham's heretical teachings came late in his ministry, and Cain has explicitly rejected Branham at those points where the latter's teaching is clearly nonbiblical.[6]

(3) I think Cain was naive in his endorsement of the Kansas City Fellowship. For example, Cain's explicit blessing of Bob Jones was a major error, given the wild and eccentric nature of Jones's teachings and claims. After Bob Jones was disciplined for major sin (involving prophetic abuses related to sexual misconduct) in the fall of 1991, I was told that Cain had never trusted Jones in the first place. While it was generous of him not to reveal his doubts, they

should have at least demanded that Cain refrain from strong approval of Jones's prophetic calling.

(4) The prophetic ministry of Cain brought a mixed blessing to the Vineyard, in spite of incredible crowds and the early adulation of Cain. There is good evidence that Cain and Wimber got their signals crossed about Cain's public prediction of a revival in Britain in 1990. Likewise, internal Vineyard prophecies made by Cain were divisive and led to serious confrontations between Wimber and some of his top aides.

(5) In both KCF and the Vineyard there has been exaggeration of Cain's status in the healing revivals of the 1950s. Cain was involved for sure, but he was not prominent like Branham, Roberts, or a host of others.

What about the suggestion that Cain rescued the Vineyard in the summer of 1988? Though he stated in his fax to me that "this is not for public information" and that "it is family business within the Vineyard," news about the supernatural rescue had already been made public in a *Charisma* cover story (September, 1989) and in David Pytches' *Some Said It Thundered*. In the former, Paul Thigpen mentions that before Wimber met Cain, "a problem situation in the internal life of the Vineyard organization had been exposed and corrected through accurate prophecy of this total stranger."[7]

Pytches' account gives more dramatic detail. He writes that Cain, while in Dallas, received "revelations from the Lord which were forwarded by telephone to John Wimber via a third party." Pytches goes on to state that Wimber was "astounded at the insight of Paul Cain who had provided him with such very perceptive information, which Paul could not possibly have gained from any human source."[8]

The situation addressed by Cain involved a political crisis, but the sad story is not helped by allusions of prophetic rescue. It is, rather, a tragic case of bungled church politics. The idea that Cain could not have had a human source for his information is nonsense. There were several people who could have been in regular contact with Cain about the very matters he raised. I know of no current

Vineyard leader who would accept the Thigpen and Pytches accounts, including John Wimber himself.

The Vineyard and the Prophetic

Despite initial enthusiasm for the prophetic in 1988, Wimber soon realized that the gift of prophecy had some serious negative aspects. While he did not abandon belief in the exercise of this gift, he gradually returned to the original emphases in the Vineyard. This meant, in part, some separation and distance from Bob Jones, Paul Cain, and Jack Deere. By 1992 Jones was associated with another group, Paul Cain became affiliated with other prophetic leaders, and Jack Deere returned to Texas as a base for a worldwide teaching ministry.

In 1993 I spent twelve hours in conversation with Mike Bickle while he was in Canada at a conference on prophecy and renewal. Mike make it clear that God had used the critique of Ernie Gruen to bring a deeper level of legitimate caution about prophecy to Kansas City. Later that same year Gruen and Bickle jointly signed a declaration of peace between their two churches.

Two final observations are appropriate about the Vineyard's involvement with the Kansas City prophets. On the one hand, it illustrates that Wimber can be vulnerable to excesses typical of charismatic Christianity. However, it also shows his ability to be self-critical and to redirect the movement once errors are detected.

Nine
Prophecy and The Toronto Blessing

For nearly two centuries Christians have been preoccupied with eschatology. An endless stream of books dealing with Bible prophecy has been published. One writer in a recent edition of *The Ambassador Report* (a newsletter on the Worldwide Church of God) complained about "the disease of apocaholism"—the obsession with apocalyptic and eschatological speculations.

But Christians do want comfort in facing the future, and prophecy offers a guide through the storms of life. It helps them see God's hand working in history, through the present, and into the future. Ultimately, nothing is more comforting than the biblical promise that the Lord Jesus will return again in triumph and glory.

Some defenders of The Toronto Blessing have strongly argued that the arrival of this phenomenon was announced ahead of time through prophecy. In fact, Randy Clark told me on the first anniversary night that the Blessing had been predicted by various prophets and that he has been gathering these prophecies from a number of sources throughout Canada and the United States. This claim has authenticated the Toronto renewal for many participants.

Different Understandings of Prophecy

As the last chapter indicated, the 1990s have seen a vigorous dispute over the gift of prophecy. Before examining the relationship of prophecy to The Toronto Blessing, we should have some knowledge of the different interpretations of prophecy.

The vast majority of Christians believe that prophecy refers to at least four things: (1) the ministry and teaching of Old Testament prophets, (2) the activity of New Testament prophets, (3) the gift of prophecy exercised in the apostolic period, and (4) the study of biblical teaching about the end times, specifically the events surrounding the return of Jesus Christ.

Most evangelical Christians also believe that the genuine Old Testament prophets were infallible or inerrant in their prophetic messages—a view based chiefly on Deuteronomy 18:22: "If what a prophet proclaims in the name of the LORD does not take place or come true, that is a message the LORD has not spoken. That prophet has spoken presumptuously. Do not be afraid of him."

In general, the church throughout history has not looked kindly on the gift of prophecy in the postapostolic period. However, there have been significant periods when Christians, both male and female, have claimed to be prophets. We are in such a time today. The Pentecostal and charismatic groups in particular have accepted the gift of prophecy, as has the Vineyard movement (see previous chapter).

There is a significant difference in the concept of a modern-day Christian prophet from the concept of the Old Testament prophet. It is widely assumed by those who believe prophecy still occurs that such prophets can make mistakes—even false prophecies. In other words, a Christian prophet can make errors just like someone who has the gift of teaching, like a good preacher who has a bad day in the pulpit, or like someone with the gift of discernment who makes an unwise judgment. In other words, the gift of prophecy today does not seem to demand inerrancy in prediction. Some writers even contend that the New Testament prophets made mistakes in prophetic speculation.

This perspective, of course, must not be reduced to absurdity. Advocates of modern-day prophecy admit that a high rate of false prophecies suggests that someone may have missed his or her calling! Likewise, all Christian prophets have to be rooted in obedience to Jesus Christ as their share in the gift of prophecy.

I am not attempting here to decide the issue of whether the gift of prophecy is for today. However, the previous chapter has made explicit how dangerous this gift can be in today's church. While it is true that any of the Spirit's gifts can be abused, there is something especially risky about the "sign" gifts, because of the drama and power that go with them.

The Nature of Powerful Prophetic Ministry

Several key issues are relevant in examining alleged prophecies of The Toronto Blessing. (1) Predictions announced *after* the fact have virtually no value. What good is it, for example, to tell someone in 1950 that the Lord told you World War II would start in 1939? That would have the same value as my telling you *now* that the Lord told me in 1982 that Bill Clinton would become the President of the United States.

(2) There is also minimal value in predictions that are *vague*. What good is a prophecy that can be stored for varied and diverse application? "I see by the word of the Lord that there will be a great renewal among his people in northern California." Or, "The Lord is warning about the unbelief in Europe."

On this matter, Rodney Howard-Browne makes some telling points against low standards in prophetic gifting. He states in his book *Flowing in the Holy Ghost*:

> Some of these counterfeit prophecies can be *hilarious*. One person got up and said, "The Lord would say unto thee, fear has come upon the land, such fear as never before, so that even I, the Lord your God, am afraid." Can you picture God on His throne with His knees knocking?[1]

He also mentions the case of a Pentecostal lady confused on her biblical terminology. "She got up and said, 'The Lord would say, I've taken my Spirit out of this church. Yea, I've written "Michelob" on the door.' The word she should have used was 'Ichabod,' not 'Michelob'! 'Ichabod' means 'the glory has departed.' Can you imagine God putting a beer advertisement on the door of a church?"[2] And he tells a third story that raises the same concern about careless prophecy. "A man got up and prophesied at length about how 'my servant Abraham led my people out of the land of Egypt.' After ten minutes, he realized something was wrong, so he added, 'The Lord would say unto thee, He's sorry He made a mistake. It wasn't Abraham; it was Moses.'"[3]

Such examples are humorous, but they make a point that deserves deep and penetrating reflection in the charismatic world. The Word of God states: "You shall not misuse the name of the LORD your God" (Ex. 20:7). This commandment from Mount Sinai is a word for modern-day prophets. It is an awesome thing to claim to speak in the name of the Holy One.

(3) A third issue is that specific and accurate prophecies must be rooted in *overall prophetic accuracy*. Whenever I teach on the New Age movement in churches, I usually do a role play of a psychic or channeler making predictions. I remember one occasion when my prophecy was right on target, and the report of it, standing alone, would sound impressive. However, that one accurate prediction stood in a field of a hundred false prophecies. True predictions lose their value if the prophet gives us only his or her best hits and keeps the misses in the closet. Anyone can make a few accurate prophecies, given enough opportunity.

(4) Finally, a prophetic gift will have *power* and *insight* that brings the spoken Word of God to our day. Tragically, this most dominant characteristic of the Old Testament prophetic literature is missing in modern Christian prophecy. Where is the Isaiah who can speak dramatically to a nation? Where is the Amos who can thunder against the wickedness of a pagan culture? Where is the Jeremiah who can pronounce wrath on false prophets?

In summary, true Christian prophets will honor their calling by announcing prophecies ahead of time, being specific and clear in the prophetic word, disclosing all prophecies so that credibility can be established, and speaking with power and insight so that people know that the Lord Almighty has spoken. If they fail to meet these high standards, then something is amiss. It is on such high standards that we must examine claims that The Toronto Blessing was foretold by modern-day prophets.

The Case of Marc Dupont

The most famous prophecy claimed as a prediction of The Toronto Blessing was given by Marc Dupont, a member of the Airport Vineyard. Marc has an international prophetic and teaching ministry. His prophetic word about Toronto is given in Chevreau's work *Catch the Fire* and is mentioned in numerous articles. Here are some of the central points of his prophetic word. I have numbered them for the sake of convenient reference.

Part One: May, 1992, for Southern Ontario

1. "Toronto shall be a place where much living water will be flowing, even though at the present time both the church and the city are like big rocks—cold and hard, [and resistant] to God's love and His Spirit."

2. "The breaking of pride and stiffness will result in Christians and churches which can fit together [like stones] in the Master Builder's hands."

3. "Many will hear the new song that God will be putting in the mouths of His people and many will come to fear the Lord."

4. "In that freedom, many churches will begin to take worship out into the public arenas, where the unchurched can hear. The artists and musicians of Toronto are going to experience a strong move[ment] of God's Spirit."

5. "[A great number of] traditional denominational pastors and churches are going to be in the forefront of the move[ment] of the Spirit that will take place."

6. "I believe that many Evangelical Pastors are going to have a tremendous prophetic anointing on their ministries and become the Lord's spokesmen to other pastors."

7. "Many current leaders will not be the leaders of the coming move, because many of them will disqualify themselves by not responding to what the Father will be saying."

8. "Like Jerusalem, Toronto will be a centre from which many are sent out to the nations, on all continents. The Lord is going to be sending [out] many people, filled with His Spirit, [who are able to] demonstrate strong giftings, vision, and love."

9. "In the move that is coming, there are going to be new Bible schools, training centres, and leadership schools raised up. These schools will have a focus not only on Bible knowledge, but also in ministries of healing the broken hearts, and setting the captives free, and on developing intimacy with the Father."

10. "I saw those waters like a strong raging river head west all the way to the Rocky Mountains, and then go north along the eastern edge of the mountains, and then go east again across the plains. In essence, there was a huge circle of water that wrapped around the plains of Canada."

Part Two: July 5, 1993: For the Present Leadership of the Body of Christ in Toronto

11. "I believe the Lord indicated that the increase in evangelism, the moving of the Holy Spirit, and the call to intercessory prayer is going to happen even this summer and autumn, with the pace accelerating into the new year."

12. "Many [leaders] will fall into temptation and sin, and will leave the ministry or bring judgment on themselves and their churches, which in turn will be greatly shaken, many to the point of falling apart."

13. "For those that begin to catch what the Spirit is saying to them, they are going to be taking radical steps that are going to be extremely [difficult] for those in the churches who are not hearing what the Spirit is saying."

14. "I also sensed from the Lord an extreme danger for leaders who continue to [resist] the Holy Spirit."

15. "The Lord is calling us to do things which are completely beyond our abilities and past experiences."

16. "There is going to be a move[ment] of the Spirit of God on the city that is going to include powerful signs and wonders, such as in the early days of the Church in Jerusalem."

17. "There are also going to be leaders raised up in the Body of Christ that are going to move in an authority that will be transdenominational."

18. "I believe that there is going to be a very strong freedom [to move in] miracles, healings, and signs and wonders, happening very consistently in the Body of Christ, and touching especially [the lives of] non-believers."[4]

Using the guidelines outlined earlier, what represents a fair and accurate response to Dupont's prophecy? First, Dupont's prophetic word was released *before* The Toronto Blessing began. Tapes of these prophecies were made well in advance of January 20, 1994. That is to his credit.

As to *specificity and accuracy*, however, my impression is that many predictions (e.g., 3, 5, 7, 9, 11, 14, 15, and 17) are either obvious judgments or are vague—some more so than others. They do not in themselves give much clarity to what was to be expected on the horizon. For example, the notion that "many will come to fear the Lord" is a safe prediction, and the prediction of the rise of an authoritative, transdenominational leadership is true in any generation.

Furthermore, seven predictions (2, 4, 6, 10, 12, 16, and 18) are either only partly true of The Blessing or have not yet taken place. The Toronto renewal has contributed to some of the unity mentioned in Prediction 2, but it has also exhibited "pride and stiffness" by its own elitism. "The artists and musicians" have yet to "experience a strong move of God's Spirit." Canada's western provinces have yet to experience renewal that would amount to something "like a strong raging river," nor have "many" churches been falling apart because of fallen "leaders." And there has been no duplication (as suggested in 16 and 18) of the miracles, healings, and signs and wonders of the early church.

This leaves, then, only three statements (1, 8, and 13) reasonably clear and specific. If one accepts The Toronto Blessing as from God, then this Canadian city has become "a place where much living water" flows. Moreover, Toronto has become "a centre from which many are sent out to the nations"—though many who are sent out are actually from other nations who have arrived in Toronto for "The Blessing." Finally, from one angle, those experiencing the Toronto renewal have taken "radical steps" that have indeed created "extreme" difficulty for people in other churches. That these steps involve uncontrollable laughing, shaking, roaring, barking, and other manifestations is not specified in the prophecy. Many Christians believe that these "radical steps" are not central or necessarily helpful for the spiritual life of the church. Of course, the prophet can always say that the Spirit warned about such unbelief!

On the bottom line, fifteen of eighteen prophecies are either general, vague, or have yet to be fulfilled. This is not a great track record on which to build certainty. While the future may bring successful closure to some of the prophecies, Christians should suspend judgment of it as a true word from the Lord.

Other Alleged Prophecies

While Marc Dupont's prophecy is the most famous, other prophecies are circulating that are said to be about The Toronto Blessing. We should examine several of these briefly. Dave Roberts mentions a work by David Obbard (a Strict Baptist pastor from Kent) who received a prophetic vision forty years ago that claimed a "revival" would start in 1994. This work, *Ploughboy to Pastor* (published privately), would certainly constitute advance notice if the prophecy was recorded in 1954.

However, a major problem with this argument is that The Toronto Blessing is not a revival, nor has it been called a revival by its leading proponents.[5] Even if we used the term *revival* in a loose sense, there is the issue of chronology. Why date the start of the "revival" as 1994? Though that is when Holy Laughter hit the Vineyard, it is certainly not the year that the "anointing" fell on Rodney Howard-Browne (1979) or radical church renewal began through his ministry in Albany, New York (1989).

Randy Clark mentioned to me that Paul Cain prophesied the outpouring in Toronto. To ascertain the accuracy of this claim, Cain must release all his prophecies in written format and circulate them before events happen. When Randy Clark told me that Cain predicted The Toronto Blessing, I asked him if he knew that he also predicted that John Wimber would be "the End-Time Apostle," leading Joel's Army. Clark had not heard this prophecy, one that Wimber rejected immediately. We should resist prophecies that are announced so readily after things have taken shape.

Bob Jones has also claimed that the Lord told him in 1984 that in ten years he would see the fruit of a mighty work of God. It has been suggested that The Toronto Blessing is a fulfillment of that word. I strongly question this on several grounds. The alleged word to Jones was a general prophecy, not a specific word about Toronto. Moreover, any prophecy from the Kansas City Fellowship must be held deeply suspect because of the things noted in the last chapter.

This 1984 prophecy must be set in its context. In March of 1983 Mike Bickle had accepted Bob Jones as a prophet of God. This was the start of a seven-year period of wild speculation, false prophecy, and unbridled elitism in the Kansas City Fellowship, and it was not until the spring and summer of 1990 that Wimber brought discipline to that church. In other words, in its context, Jones's 1984 prophecy does not deserve to be considered a prediction from the Lord about Toronto.

Toronto's Prophetic Spirit

In my view, the evidence that God foretold The Toronto Blessing through his prophets is not convincing. I welcome criticism of my viewpoint, but the burden clearly lies on Toronto Blessing defenders to restate their case. What is needed here is proof that such prophecies are given ahead of time, with clarity, and in the context of overall accuracy.

The above points lead to three final observations about prophecy as it relates to The Toronto Blessing. (1) There is something problematic with the self-referential focus of the alleged prophecies. Is this an indication of the Canadian psyche that needs to prove itself? Christians once wrote long books to prove that England and America were in prophecy. Must we now do the same for Canada?

(2) The prophetic ministry in Toronto lacks profound depth and power. In contrast to Old Testament prophecy, this modern version is rather limited in its scope and insight. It is no wonder that a recent work states:

> A prophetic ministry that springs out of the exposition of the Scriptures is less likely to become volatile and ensnared in mystical subjectivism. A prophetic ministry that addresses the issues of an unjust world is less likely to become in-house entertainment for the saints. For the contemporary charismatic, there is the need to be willing to make and stand by responsible theological judgements concerning what is good for the mission of Christ, rather than to feel that because pronouncements are made in an authoritative and subjective fashion they must carry more weight. Discernment has as much to do with careful thought and theological analysis as with inspired guesses and sudden intuitions.[6]

One of the saddest characteristics of modern-day prophecy is how distinctively weak it is in contrast to the Old Testament prophets. This point applies to the Vineyard movement as it has embraced the prophetic since 1988. When one reads either the Kansas City or The Toronto Blessing prophets, it is obvious that we are not being offered penetrating prophetic analysis that speaks to the heart of our culture.

These modern prophecies do not give God's searing rebuke to the political ideologies of our day. Moreover, they do not even speak powerfully against their own church traditions. Both in Kansas City and in Toronto, the prophets spend too much of their time defending everything at home base, while issuing the occasional spiritual death threats to critics. In short, from this perspective, these modern prophets do not sound like prophets at all.

How should we explain, then, the adoration and fascination of the charismatic multitudes with these modern-day prophets? There are several factors. (a) Such adulation is a commentary on how little time Christians give to a penetrating study of the Old Testament prophets. Given this neglect, it is easy to be impressed by a far weaker model.

(b) What fascinates many Christians is the supernatural and mystical tales (usually in the private domain) of God's interaction with the prophet. For example, charismatic crowds revel in accounts of trips to heaven, trips to hell, angelic visitations, overt demonic warfare, and so forth. At the Kansas City Fellowship, the congregations used to get excited when Bob Jones and John Paul Jackson said that they could see each other's angel! No one else could see angels, but the multitudes were still thrilled.

(c) Christians have few places to turn for powerful prophetic analysis of modern culture. It is lamentable that the evangelical tradition has lost its voice in the public square. Fortunately, there are at least a few examples to cite as a guide for powerful prophetic ministry. One thinks immediately of Charles Colson and his penetrating indictment of the current state of world affairs. Colson serves well as a prophetic voice because he knows what the real world is like, given his years of experience not only in the Nixon government but in the world of prison ministry.

Let me mention two other examples. Many articles in the *New York Review of Books* offer a superb critique of the ills and evils of our world. Likewise, the editorial page of the *New York Times* often provides stunning commentary on our world. For example, if you read the columns of A. M. Rosenthal, one of the senior editors at the *New York Times*, you will be struck by the power, range, and prophetic nature of his columns. Perhaps, in God's mysterious ways, Rosenthal has picked up from his Jewish heritage the rich and deep understanding of what it means to speak as a prophet in a world gone mad.

(3) Finally, the most tragic element in The Toronto Blessing is the reckless and divisive prophecies delivered from the Airport Vineyard pulpit. For example, at the October, 1994, "Catch the Fire" conference, Wes Campbell alluded to a 1984 prophetic warning from Bob Jones about a "bloody civil war" in the church. Campbell went on to refer to an alleged prophecy from James Ryle about the war between the "blue coats" (standing for the revelatory) and the "grey coats" (standing for "grey matter, man's wisdom").[7]

The first issue of *Spread the Fire* contains a prophecy from Stacey Campbell that delivers a thunderous warning on the need to "Choose! Choose! Choose!" about The Toronto Blessing while we are "in the days of power, and in the days of sight when many miraculous things are being done." The prophecy announces wrath on those who cause division. "It will be better for Sodom and Gomorrah than it will be for that one on that day." Readers are then told they have a choice: Accept The Toronto Blessing and "call it 'God' or follow after human wisdom and reasoning." The prophecy ends with the question, "Is it God or isn't it?"

What is fundamentally wrong here is not only the coercive language but its dualistic thrust. Furthermore, it is precisely this kind of prophetic carelessness that causes division. If The Toronto Blessing is to be accepted as being of God, surely an appeal rooted in love will do far more than this kind of rhetoric.

Wes and Stacey Campbell are passionate leaders in the Vineyard. The Christian church needs more of their zeal and radical commitment. However, the church will not be brought into unity through divisive prophecy. These words were given after only eight months into the renewal. Why the rush to judgment?

Such prophetic warnings also fail since they cause division on secondary issues. Christians are not alarmed by the Vineyard's call for renewal. That is, no one in the body of Christ is upset that the gospel is being preached at the Airport Vineyard. Rather, the debate is mainly about the strange manifestations, ones that have caused even John Wimber some puzzlement. Do we really need warnings about Sodom and Gomorrah over these items?

In November 1994 Larry Randolph said:

> There is not a lot of neutral ground. The neutral ground is dissipating by the hour. You can't stand in the middle any more and say, "Well, I don't know. Maybe it's God, maybe it's not." You're going to get rolled over. Remember the song "I'm a Steam Roller, Baby, And I'm Going To Roll Right Over You"? Well, I think the Holy Spirit is singing that song. There is no middle ground.[8]

Randolph has also said that God told him that Jesus himself is going to appear in churches before the end of this millennium.[9]

John White, the well-known Christian psychiatrist, has announced his calling as a prophet. He has recently stated that "terrible judgment is coming on the church, particularly in Ontario."[10] Given John White's error about those who dared to question the Kansas City prophets, his latest round of rumblings has a rather hollow ring to it. Hopefully, as the months pass, there will be less exhibition of this prophetic immaturity.

Ten

Biblical Faith and The Toronto Blessing

I mentioned earlier that further probing The Toronto Blessing with regard to "the biblical test" is necessary. I also suggested that in any such analysis, we should not claim that the Vineyard in general is "unbiblical." In evangelical Protestant circles one can hardly issue a stronger judgment against a particular person or group than to say, "They do not believe the Bible."

Since the time of the Reformation a consensus has emerged among evangelicals as to what constitutes the "heart" of biblical faith. A firm commitment to certain central biblical convictions brings fundamental unity with other Christians. In the last several decades, there has also been recognition of common ground between orthodox Catholics and evangelical Protestants on the core principles of biblical revelation.

The Association of Vineyard Churches stands in solid agreement with other Christian groups on the central and classic themes of Holy Scripture. Given this, whatever misuse, neglect, or misinterpretation of the Bible takes place out of The Toronto Blessing should be raised in "good faith" to Vineyard leaders and others. Similarly, Vineyard members and Toronto Blessing participants have every right to speak about their concerns and criticisms in regard to failings concerning Scripture that they observe in other denominational groups.

This methodological point needs brief elaboration. What tempts many Protestants is a hypocritical use of the Bible as a sword to critique *others*. Since "the word of God is living and active" and "sharper than any double-edged sword" (Heb. 4:12), the Bible's powerful message must be applied self-referentially. This is the context of Jesus' famous remark: "Do not judge, or you too will be judged" (Matt. 7:1).

While I was doing research for my book *Crisis of Allegiance*, a study about Jehovah's Witnesses, I read Timothy White's *A People for His Name*, a brilliant analysis of the Watch Tower Society. White makes this judgment:

> A distressing feature of the Witnesses' criticism of others is their breaking of the sound law of Deuteronomy 25:13, "Thou shalt not have in thy bag divers weights, a great and a small," that is, they attach far more weight to a fault in another organization than the same fault in their own. Thus the false doctrine of Christendom is inexcusable, but the same thing in Russell is dimly-shining light. Crimes in Christendom show the Churches cannot be of God, but crimes in the New World Society, if they are acknowledged at all, are merely the results of human imperfection which we should not allow to stumble us.[1]

If The Toronto Blessing is too wild, are not dead and boring services an equal, if not greater, sin? If Vineyard leaders put too much emphasis on spiritual "experiences," what about other church leaders who deny them completely? If the Holy Spirit is overemphasized, what shall we say against churches that ignore the Spirit?

Positive Biblical Patterns

I want to begin by pointing out several healthy aspects to the scriptural focus of The Toronto Blessing. (1) I admire John Arnott's repeated *exaltation of God's power*. He constantly states that "we should have more faith in God's power to bless us than in Satan's ability to deceive us." This quote should not be twisted, of course, as some have done, to suggest that John does not believe in discernment or that he does not know or care about Satan's cunning (cf. 2 Cor. 11:14).

(2) The Toronto Blessing is picking up on the rich teaching of Scripture that the Christian church is in constant *need of renewal*. In one way, the Vineyard's current phase represents, at its best, something similar to the call of John Wesley to the church of his day. As Wesley knew, it is singularly clear from the Law of Moses (Deut. 30:6) through to the Apocalypse of John (Rev. 2:4) that the "heart" of God's people is of utmost concern to humanity's Creator.[2] The importance of the experience of the Spirit cannot be denied. As James Dunn writes:

> That the Spirit, and particularly the gift of the Spirit, was a fact of experience in the lives of the earliest Christians has been too obvious to require elaboration. It is a sad commentary on the poverty of our own immediate experience of the Spirit that when we come across language in which the NT writers refer directly to the gift of the Spirit and to their experience of it, either we automatically refer it to the sacraments and can only give it meaning when we do so, or else we discount the experience described as too subjective and mystical in favour of a faith which is essentially an affirmation of biblical propositions, or else we in effect psychologize the Spirit out of existence.[3]

(3) The Toronto Blessing is also about *evangelism and revival*, central themes of Scripture (Matt. 28:18–20). Some critics have said unjustly that the Airport Vineyard leaders do not care about mission. This is simply false, as evidenced by the significant number who have become Christians in this renewal movement. In terms of social outreach, the Airport Vineyard has regular programs involving Christian compassion to the poor and the homeless. In a recent edition of the Vineyard newsletter, *Spread the Fire* (March-April, 1995), there is a dramatic story about the social and evangelistic empowerment that Ace Clarke (a former member of the Wild Ones motorcycle gang) received at the October, 1994, "Catch the Fire" Conference.[4]

(4) The Airport Vineyard leaders have been exemplary in their *lack of focus on money* (Matt. 6:19–34). They have not given into the temptation to pressure the large crowds into handing over their wallets. I remember my first visit to a large charismatic rally when I was a teenager. It was under the "Big Tent," and the healing evangelist had a vision of the exact numbers in the crowd who would give a specific amount of cash, and he kept the offering going until the "Lord" was pleased!

(5) The Toronto Blessing is *nonlegalistic* in its ethos and style. Jesus warned against mean and uptight religion in his rebuke to certain Jewish leaders of his day (Matt. 23:1–36). One of the appeals of the Vineyard movement has been its relaxed style. This ease of spirit must be applauded and should not be dismissed as indifference, laziness, or antinomianism.

These five important, positive elements (and more could be mentioned) should serve as a clear signal that The Toronto Blessing is fundamentally about Christian living under obedience to God's Word. Whatever criticisms we may make of unbiblical aspects to the Vineyard (even, or especially, in its latest phase) must be set in fundamental recognition of its essential desire to be based on Scripture.

Of course, there are groups that claim to have a high regard for the Scriptures and yet obviously know little about the truths of the Bible. I think here, for example, of the Mormon church, Jehovah's Witnesses, New Age religion, or the Unification Church of Sun Myung Moon. These groups are labeled cultic because of this very dichotomy.

As I have studied the Vineyard over the past four years, I am convinced that its leaders want to be scriptural in their theology and practice. Biblical authority is not an issue that separates the Vineyard from other denominations. If Vineyard pastors are approached with evidence that the Bible is not being obeyed, such criticism will be taken seriously.

In fact, in the course of research, I have felt that a couple of actions made against me by several Toronto Vineyard leaders were unbiblical in both substance and method. It took only a few minutes of probing this issue with the relevant leaders for things to be corrected, including acknowledgment on my part of some errors in judgment. It was on the basis of common ground in Scripture that these issues were resolved.

Critical Biblical Concerns

Having just listed five positive points of the Vineyard movement, I move now to an equal number of critical concerns about the misuse of Scripture in relation to The Toronto Blessing. I do not believe that my judgments here are unbalanced or picky. In fact, attention to these pivotal issues will prove the extent to which Vineyard leaders are open to full biblical counsel.

(1) Something should be done about the *weak preaching* that typifies the nightly meetings. I have talked to hundreds of people who have been to the Airport Vineyard and have asked them about their perceptions of the strengths and weaknesses of the preaching they heard. Their chief complaint is the lack of clarity, exegetical skill, and focus that is brought to the biblical text during worship.

Since October, 1994, I have attended about thirty meetings. My view matches the majority opinion I have heard from others, including my colleagues at Ontario Theological Seminary. A regular pattern has emerged since January 20, 1994, in that the messages usually consist of story-telling about "manifestations" or about the latest developments in The Blessing. Biblical proclamation has not emerged as a keystone of this renewal. For that there needs to be serious adjustment, quickly.

(2) The Toronto Blessing offers *a reductionistic view of the Holy Spirit.*[5] Here is one of the chief ironies of The Toronto Blessing. Its defenders claim that it is a mighty outpouring of the Spirit, but this alleged great move of God is also hampered by a rather shallow doctrine of pneumatology. Since critics may make fun of the words "doctrine" or "pneumatology," let me state this point another way: The view of the Holy Spirit that flows out of this Toronto renewal is, paradoxically, a weak and limiting one.

The failure here has nothing to do with the power of the Spirit. Who can doubt the explosive dynamism of God's Spirit? Likewise, their inadequate view of the Spirit has little to do with whether or not God is doing wonderful things at the Toronto Vineyard. I firmly believe that the Spirit is at work, often in significant ways. Rather, the frailty in the current Toronto view has to do with the feeble interpretation of the Spirit that flows as a central but unnecessary current from this renewal.

Consider, for example, the question posed in the *Charisma* cover story on The Toronto Blessing: "What Is God Doing in Toronto?" The short answer to this question is that God is *finally* working in this great Canadian city. The fundamental but pathetic posture of The Toronto Blessing is that God is doing *only one* thing in Toronto: His Spirit is being poured out at the Airport Vineyard. Period. End of story.

Of course, no one in leadership in the Airport Vineyard is going to admit to this reductionistic view. And in all good conscience, they may deny my criticism. But my point is not about what is explicitly taught or consciously thought. Rather, it is about implicit but obvious teachings, about unconscious but undeniable assumptions.

The reductionist view of the Spirit can be illustrated in a host of ways. Even a casual glance through transcripts of evening messages illustrates a self-absorbed ideology at work. Moreover, the hasty jeremiads against critics are proof of a narrow view of the Spirit. Vineyard leaders are also too ready to bless everything they do and expect that the rest of the Christian church will fall in line.

It has been wonderful to hear from many people about the great renewal God has brought to them through The Toronto Blessing. It is equally painful to have heard from many people from all denominations of the ways that devotees of the Vineyard renewal have manifested an unspiritual pushiness about the latest ride on the Third Wave. A friend of mine from California was told that this is the greatest move of God on earth and that he *must* get on a plane to Toronto.

There are a lot of God-fearing, Bible-believing, and Spirit-filled Christians in southern Ontario who will *not* go to the Airport Vineyard precisely because of this shallow view of God's alleged workings. One mission worker in Toronto phoned me to tell how divisive Vineyard leaders had been in a cooperative retreat: "It was the Vineyard way or no way."

In Toronto and elsewhere, churches are splitting over the "manifestations." Marriages are being divided over shaking and lion roaring. Much productive time is lost in mission and evangelism because of needless animosity, too much of it created by The Toronto Blessing's unhelpful attitude that it is the only show in Canada. Clark Pinnock, a theologian openly supportive of The Toronto Blessing, has also expressed concerns at this point.

The Spirit of God landed in Toronto long before January 20, 1994. In thousands of churches and in a million ways, the Holy Spirit has been working in this great Canadian city. We should praise God for every blessing that has come and will come from his sovereign and mighty work out of the Airport Vineyard. This praise will be only diminished if it is based on a shallow and limiting view of the Spirit, one that dares to suggest that the supernatural God is stuck in a rut on the Vineyard runway.

(3) Contrary to the Bible, The Toronto Blessing has *an anti-intellectual spirit*. To many Christians, this would be a badge of honor. After all, is it not every believer's duty to avoid worldly wisdom (1 Cor. 1:18–25)? Does not the apostle Paul say that we should "demolish arguments and every pretension that sets itself up against the knowledge of God, and [that] we take captive every thought to make it obedient to Christ" (2 Cor. 10:5)?

The answer to these rhetorical questions is obvious. My third concern is not about these clear truths. Rather, one of the disappointing manifestations of The Toronto Blessing is a disregard for real wisdom at too many points. Airport Vineyard leaders and teachers have not "taken every thought" captive to Christ. The anti-intellectual spirit is dominant. There is a price to pay for sloppy thought, careless claims, and foolish rhetoric. That price may not be at the level of numbers. If wisdom is proven by big crowds, then The Toronto Blessing has all the marks of genius. Great body count does not determine wisdom, however. I hope that the multitudes continue to come to Toronto for renewal. Insofar as many people travel to distant places for physical renewal on holidays, vacations, retreats, etc., we should not complain when people make a pilgrimage to Toronto for eternal value.

But the "eternal weight of glory" (to use C. S. Lewis's phrase) demands deeper and more penetrating discernment from Toronto Blessing exponents. Jesus regretted that unbelievers are sometimes wiser than the children of light. Paul warned against a zeal "not based on knowledge" (Rom. 10:2). Peter instructed us to add "knowledge" to our "faith" and "goodness" (2 Peter 1:5).

What evidence justifies this third concern? Several factors come to mind. Apologists for The Toronto Blessing give the impression that Christians should not judge the renewal. James Ryle has warned against "watchdogs of doctrinal purity" who are now offering criticism of the Vineyard.[6] Granted, much criticism of the Vineyard and Rodney Howard-Browne has been severe. But this criticism will not be easily muted as long as apologists like Ryle or William DeArteaga make their own severe judgments on those who dare to question the movement.

There should be concern about the total ease with which virtually every aspect of The Toronto Blessing has been defended here in Toronto. It is disappointing when John Arnott says in an interview that he has no regrets about anything connected with the renewal. Can it really be that good? What about the divine death threats delivered by Vineyard prophets? What about the wildest of the manifestations? Is it all of God?

Vineyard leaders need to tone down their complaints against theology, acting as if the disciplined study of Christian doctrine is an intrinsic evil. The constant snide remarks against the intellect are distressing, as is the steady drip of negativity about other churches. The simplistic endorsement of "experience" is naive. In regard to their failure to achieve theological balance and precision, R. T.

Kendall, pastor of Westminster Chapel, is a better guide. He has been touched by this renewal, but he refuses to duplicate the anti-intellectualism of many Blessing apologists.

The one great irony in the anti-intellectualism that manifests itself too readily is that this goes side by side with the constant invocation of Jonathan Edwards as the guiding light for this renewal. This man's intellectual rigor, his passion for careful theology, his precision in analysis, and his longing for penetrating discernment should raise hope that the irrational impulses in The Toronto Blessing will be reduced as Vineyard leaders listen more readily to his voice, one that combined renewal of intellect and spirit in a remarkable way.

(4) The Toronto Blessing represents a *faulty understanding of signs and wonders*. This, like the second criticism, is paradoxical, especially since the Vineyard movement is known for its expertise on the topic. However, this current renewal is less than fully biblical in its views of miracles.

This is not to say that those in the Vineyard err in their longing for signs and wonders. Who can fault the sick who want divine healing? Who can question the blind who want sight? Who can blame anyone who wants deliverance from demonic bondage? Even the wildest beliefs that God might bring someone back from the dead deserve our sympathy. Thus, the charismatic yearning for the miraculous is not unbiblical.

What is inadequate in The Toronto Blessing is that its defenders use the term *miracle* too readily about this renewal. The weakness here is twofold. (a) It amounts to unintended false advertising about itself. I have talked with many people who expected to be astounded when they arrived for their first meeting, but were disappointed by what they saw. Possibly many others who have made the long journey to Toronto have had to fight deep feelings of regret that their experience did not match the rhetoric they heard in advance. Obviously, of course, I admit that there are many others who have found the Airport Vineyard to be everything they had expected.

(b) More important, those who long for signs and wonders are too easily impressed by realities that are far from being powerful evidence of the miraculous. Consider again the issue of the "manifestations." Are they proof of the supernatural outpouring of the Holy Spirit? Not at all. None of the manifestations associated with The Toronto Blessing are inherently miraculous. Each one of them can be imitated by most people. An actor could be hired to attend an evening meeting and imitate all the manifestations, and no one would be able to distinguish that person from others under the "real" anointing.

Too much about the manifestations can be explained psychologically to give them much credit as signals of a supernatural touch from God. The very fact that they are duplicated in non-Christian religions strengthens my argument, though that parallel does not prove either that both groups operate out of some common psychic power or that Satan is imitating in other traditions what God is doing in the Vineyard.

Since laughing, crying, moaning, screaming, roaring, and shaking are natural human actions, such "manifestations" should be more readily explained by reference to emotional and spiritual needs on the part of the persons involved. They do not easily serve as evidence for the claim that God is doing mighty miracles in the Toronto Vineyard. I think John Wimber's approach, that these are human responses to God, is a better and more sophisticated interpretation.

What I am trying to preserve here is the biblical perspective that *miracle* involves an intrinsically supernatural component. There is a price to pay by lowering our standards of what constitutes a miracle. Jesus astonished the people of his day simply because he could do that which was, in ordinary terms, impossible. He was not afraid to prove his credentials in the eternal realm (like forgiveness of sins) by showing his power in the earthly, visible realm (like curing the sick or raising the dead).

This criticism is not intended to understate God's real work in The Toronto Blessing. Rather, my aim is to urge Vineyard leaders not to diminish the concept of miracle by easy and simplistic adoption of the popular view that the manifestations so readily show the supernatural hand of God. This isue is far too subtle and complex for that argument to have much credibility.

(5) A final criticism relates to a *lack of emphasis on the person of Christ*. Some qualifications are in order. This is not saying that Airport Vineyard leaders or those who endorse The Toronto Blessing do not care about Jesus. Nor does this mean that the lack of emphasis is unique to the Vineyard. Rather, this movement has overemphasized pneumatology to the neglect of Christology.

This is, of course, one of the major weaknesses in the charismatic tradition as a whole. In love with the things of the Spirit, its adherents have manifested a lack of focus on Jesus Christ. As is often pointed out by noncharismatic critics, this neglect of Jesus is ironic, seeing that the Spirit's role is to point us to our Lord (John 15:26). J. I. Packer comments that the charismatic movement's "intellectual and devotional preoccupation with the Holy Spirit tends to separate him from the Son whom he was sent to glorify and the Father to whom the Son brings us."[7] Tom Smail worries about

> charismatic people whose whole talk is of words of knowledge, of deliverance from evil, being slain in the Spirit, or tingling hands and high emotions at great charismatic gatherings, till one is left wondering to what extent such preoccupations bring us nearer to the heart of the New Testament gospel and to what extent they distract and divert us from it.[8]

True, those of us in noncharismatic traditions have our own sins on the same matter. In fact, we sometimes neglect both the Spirit and Jesus Christ. Sometimes our denominational pecularities get the focus instead of Christ. Our criticism, then, must be seen in this greater context. But the point still must be made for the sake of a more penetrating renewal in the Vineyard or in the ministry of Rodney Howard-Browne. Has the charismatic world lost sight of the highest priority in its rush to get the latest experience of the Spirit?

What evidence justifies this final criticism? At least two lines converge to illustrate the point. (a) Bob Hunter has analyzed by computer the focus of sermons preached in the nightly meetings at the Airport Vineyard over a three-month period. He discovered that there were 143 references to Jesus, 372 to prophecy, and 383 to the Spirit. In other words, the content of the sermons is clearly concentrated more on the Spirit than on Jesus Christ. Even prophecy and prophetic ministry are given more focus than the Messiah. This is no picky point about word games. It is about a lost opportunity in the preaching to give clear focus on the Son of God.

(b) Consider those who give their time to the "manifestations" instead of radical obsession with knowing Jesus Christ. To those who bark like a dog in worship, one might ask: Would they not do more spiritual good to themselves reading the Gospel of John? To those who spend hours shaking, one wonders: Why not spend this time in prayer with the Lord? Those who bounce like pogo sticks should ask themselves: Would not my time be better spent in direct mission for Christ, even if it means sharing, as Paul did, in the fellowship of Christ's sufferings?

On this latter point, Tom Smail writes:

> The Spirit can use a Christian community that has begun to love even a little in the way Jesus loved on the cross far more than He can use people who may have sensational experiences and dramatic gifts in plenty, but who do not know how to love in this way.[9]

Since Luther rightly noted that "the only glory of Christians is in Christ alone,"[10] the power of The Toronto Blessing or any other spiritual movement lies in direct proportion to the place given to the centrality of Christ. Ultimately, full biblical faith hinges on the identity and significance attached to our Lord. To this end, The Toronto Blessing will be a greater blessing as Christ becomes more and more central in the renewal.

Epilogue

As this book goes to press, the nightly meetings continue at Toronto's Airport Vineyard. Pilgrims arrive every week from all over the world and are met by the faithful members of the ministry teams, who seek to share with them the good news of God's love in Jesus and the touch of God's Spirit. Rodney Howard-Browne also continues his worldwide ministry. He traveled to South Africa in April, 1995, and he returns in June, 1995, for further campaigns of renewal. His humor, pointed preaching, and call for deeper Spirit-filled living continue to attract thousands.

As much as I have been critical of many aspects of Holy Laughter and The Toronto Blessing, I would be disappointed if the renewal meetings shut down. I would also be sad to hear that Rodney Howard-Browne stopped preaching. How can I say this in light of my strong concerns expressed throughout this investigative report? Basically, both the Vineyard movement and Rodney Howard-Browne have been offered a window of opportunity in God's providence to influence thousands with the gospel of Jesus Christ, a message that is full of power and vitality for the hungry and searching soul. This gospel is a story of the dramatic works of the Holy Spirit. Since Vineyard leaders and Howard-Browne know that gospel, then my hope is that they will more fully embrace all that God can do in and through their ministries.

If we think back to the five interpretations of The Toronto Blessing outlined in chapter 1, it should be obvious that I adopt no extreme position about the Airport Vineyard or Rodney Howard-Browne. I am not inclined to interpret these movements with an eschatological paradigm, pro or con. Neither am I convinced that either reality represents something unbelievably bad from the hand of Satan.

Fundamentally, neither The Toronto Blessing or the Holy Laughter revival should be understood as something without parallel in the work of God today. Rather, both realities are simply two ways among countless others that God uses to manifest his gracious and creative salvific work through Jesus Christ, our only Savior and Lord. The notion that the Holy Laughter revival or The Toronto Blessing represents something unique derives more from wishful thinking and an erroneous theology of the Spirit than anything else. One can properly recognize every wonderful aspect of both movements without giving into the temptation to elitism and self-absorption, something that manifests so often in famous renewal movements.

Since the fall of 1991, when I interviewed John Wimber, I have never forgotten his interpretation of weaknesses in the Vineyard movement. He alluded to Paul's theology as he talked about the mixture of flesh and spirit, good and bad, truth and error, that summarizes the story of the Vineyard and every other work of human beings trying to live in obedience to God. In other words, Wimber was recognizing, with Scripture, that the gospel treasure is carried in weak human vessels, so that the glory belongs to God alone (2 Cor. 4:6–7). Recognizing that fundamental point will help each of us as we seek to catch the fire of the Holy Spirit in our lives and in our churches.

NOTES

Chapter One: The Holy Spirit Has Landed

1. Robert Hough, "God Is Alive and Well and Saving Souls on Dixon Road," *Toronto Life Magazine* (February, 1995), p. 31.
2. Paul Carden, "Toronto Blessing Stirs Worldwide Controversy, Rocks Vineyard Movement," *Christian Research Journal* (Winter, 1995), p. 5.

Chapter Two: Testing the Spirits

1. Ronald Enroth, *Churches That Abuse* (Grand Rapids: Zondervan, 1992).
2. Ken Blue, *Healing Spiritual Abuse: How to Break Free from Bad Church Experiences* (Downers Grove, Ill.: InterVarsity, 1993).
3. MacArthur, *Reckless Faith* (Wheaton, Ill.: Crossway Books, 1994), p. xiii.

Chapter Three: John Wimber and the Vineyard

1. See James A. Beverley, "John Wimber, the Vineyard and the Prophets," *The Canadian Baptist* (March-April 1992), pp. 32–38. I have borrowed verbatim from that article for this chapter.
2. See the discussion in Tom Smail, Andrew Walker, and Nigel Wright, *The Love of Power or the Power of Love* (Minneapolis: Bethany, 1994).
3. James Montgomery Boice's critique of the Vineyard contains some significant inaccuracies about Wimber's relationship to Fuller. See Boice's comments in Michael Scott Horton, *Power Religion* (Chicago: Moody, 1992), pp. 119–36, and the response from Wayne Grudem, *Power and Truth* (Anaheim: Association of Vineyard Churches, 1993), p. 31.
4. See Kevin Springer, ed., *Riding the Third Wave* (Basingstoke, UK: Marshall Pickering, 1987), back cover.
5. See Grudem, *Power and Truth*, pp. 59–61.
6. See Grudem's response to Armstrong in *The Vineyard's Response to The Standard* (Anaheim: Association of Vineyard Churches, 1992). *The Standard* refused to publish any reply from Grudem (see Grudem's comments in *Power and Truth*, p. 57).
7. See letter from Reid Fowler, *The Canadian Baptist* (July-August 1992), p. 34.
8. The doctrinal statement can be obtained by writing The Association of Vineyard Churches, Box 17580, Anaheim, Calif., 92817–7580.

9. See *Equipping the Saints* (Fall 1988), with articles by Doug Groothuis and Brooks Alexander, among others. Wimber himself has an article on use of the Bible against New Age movements.

10. See Wimber's comments in *Power Healing* (San Francisco: Harper, 1987), pp. 13–20.

11. See John MacArthur, *Charismatic Chaos* (Grand Rapids: Zondervan, 1992), p. 132.

12. David Lewis, *Healing: Fiction, Fantasy or Fact?* (London: Hodder & Stoughton, 1989).

13. Wimber, in *Riding the Third Wave*, p. 31.

14. In *Philosophers Who Believe*, Alvin Plantinga talks candidly about his own feelings of superiority from his Reformed background. See his remarks in Kelly James Clark, ed., *Philosophers Who Believe* (Downers Grove, Ill.: Inter-Varsity, 1993), pp. 57–59.

15. Jack Deere, *The Vineyard's Response to* The Briefing (Anaheim: Association of Vineyard Churches, 1992).

Chapter Four: The Holy Ghost Bartender

1. *Charisma* magazine did a cover story on him in 1994. See Julia Duin, "Pass the New Wine," *Charisma* (August, 1994), pp. 20–28.

2. Rodney Howard-Browne, *The Touch of God* (Louisville, Ky.: RHBEA Publications, 1992).

3. Rodney Howard-Browne, *Flowing in the Holy Ghost* (Louisville, Ky: RHBEA Publications, 1993), p. 73.

4. Alan Morrison, "How the 'Toronto Blessing' Came to Town," *Evangelical Times* (November, 1994), p. 17.

5. Dave Roberts, *The Toronto Blessing* (Eastbourne: Kingsway, 1994), p. 113.

6. See Hank Hanegraaff, *Christianity in Crisis* (Eugene, Ore.: Harvest House, 1993), pp. 59–276.

7. Ibid., p. 14.

8. Stephen Strang, "Bridge Builders or Stone Throwers," *Charisma* (August, 1993).

9. See D. R. McConnell, *A Different Gospel* (Peabody, Mass.: Hendrickson, 1988), pp. 6–12.

10. See William DeArteaga, *Quenching the Spirit* (Lake Mary, Fla.: Creation House, 1992), p. 228.

11. This is also Hagin's answer to the charge that he borrowed extensively from a book by John A. MacMillan; see the discussion in McConnell, *A Different Gospel*, pp. 69–71.

12. C. S. Lewis, *Fern-seed and Elephants* (Glasgow: Fontana, 1975), p. 111.

Chapter Five: The Manifest Presence of Christ?

1. See comments in Guy Chevreau, *Catch the Fire* (London: HarperCollins, 1994), pp. 178–79.
2. Ibid., pp. 13–14.
3. Ibid., op. cit., p. 19.
4. Dave Roberts, *The Toronto Blessing* (Eastbourne: Kingsway Publications, 1994), p. 13.
5. Quoted in ibid., p. 32.
6. Ron Stringer, quoted in ibid., pp. 45–46.
7. Gail Reid, "After the Laughter," *Faith Today* (March/April, 1995), p. 20.
8. Diana Doucet, "What is God Doing in Toronto?" *Charisma* (February, 1995), p. 26.
9. Millar, quoted in Roberts, *The Toronto Blessing*, p. 29.
10. Kendall, quoted in ibid., p. 41.
11. Allen, quoted in Chevreau, *Catch the Fire*, p. 154.
12. William DeArteaga, *Quenching the Spirit* (Lake Mary, Fla.: Creation House, 1992), p. 55.
13. Ibid., p. 83.
14. For sophisticated analysis of intellectual thought leading up to the Enlightenment, consult Richard Popkin, *The Rise of Skepticism* (Berkeley and Los Angeles: University of California Press, 1979).
15. Chevreau, *Catch the Fire*, p. 68.
16. Ibid., p. 70.
17. Edwards, in ibid., p. 86.
18. Ibid., p. 90.
19. Ibid., p. 91.
20. This is Chevreau's wording about Chauncy (see ibid., p. 113).
21. Ibid., p. 114.
22. The sermon was printed in 1742. For selections from Tennent's book, see Robert L. Ferm, ed., *Issues in American Protestantism* (New York: Doubleday, 1969), pp. 73–83, and Edwin Scott Gaustad, ed., *Religious Issues in American History* (New York: Harper & Row, 1968), pp. 30–36. Tennent later apologized "for the excessive heat of temper which has sometimes appeared in my conduct" (see his comments in a letter in Ferm, op. cit., p. 90).
23. Chevreau, *Catch the Fire*, p. 114.
24. On Chauncy, see William DeArteaga, *Quenching the Spirit*, pp. 45–57.
25. See the remarks in Sydney E. Ahlstrom, *A Religious History of the American People* (New York: Image, 1972), Volume 1, p. 355.
26. Edwards, quoted in *Catch the Fire*, pp. 94–95.
27. Ibid., p. 101.

28. Ibid., pp. 109–10.
29. Ibid., p. 143.
30. Ibid., p. 125.
31. See Iain H. Murray's review in *The Banner of Truth* (March, 1995), pp. 28–29, emphasis his.
32. See Wimber, "Refreshing, Renewal and Revival," *Vineyard Reflections* (July-August, 1994), pp. 1–7.
33. See Wimber, "Introducing Prophetic Ministry," *Equipping the Saints* (Fall, 1990), p. 30.
34. See *Board Report*, Association of Vineyard Churches (September-October, 1994), p. 4.

Chapter Six: Lying Signs and Wonders?

1. John F. MacArthur, *Charismatic Chaos* (Grand Rapids: Zondervan, 1992), p. 40.
2. John F. MacArthur, *Reckless Faith* (Wheaton, Ill.: Crossway Books, 1994).
3. Unless otherwise noted, quotations from Hanegraaff are from his tape, "The Counterfeit Revival" (available from Christian Research Institute, Box 500, San Juan Capistrano, Calif., 92675).
4. For documentation, see the magnificent study by Paul Boyer, *When Time Shall Be No More* (Cambridge: Harvard University Press, 1992), particularly chapters 1 and 2.
5. For a careful biblical defense of premillennialism see William Sanford LaSor, *The Truth About Armageddon* (San Francisco: Harper & Row, 1982).
6. Note the comments by Richard Longenecker on Acts 2:7 in his commentary in *The Expositor's Bible Commentary* (Grand Rapids: Zondervan, 1981), vol. 9, p. 272.
7. Gordon Fee, *The First Epistle to the Corinthians* (Grand Rapids: Eerdmans, 1987), p. 697.
8. John Arnott, from a sermon at a Pastor's Meeting (Airport Vineyard, October 19, 1994).
9. Ian Rennie, Letter to the editor, *Faith Today* (September-October, 1994), p. 10.

Chapter Seven: Three Healing Cases

1. Among others, Merrill F. Unger takes this position in *The Baptism and Gifts of the Holy Spirit* (Chicago: Moody, 1974), pp. 141–42.
2. See F. David Farnell, "When Will the Gift of Prophecy Cease?" *Bibliotheca Sacra* (April–June, 1993), pp. 171–202.
3. Gordon Fee, *The First Epistle to the Corinthians* (Grand Rapids: Eerdmans, 1987), p. 645.

4. Ibid., p. 645, note 23. Fee goes on to state: "The Spirit, not Western rationalism, makes the turning of the ages, after all; and to deny the Spirit's manifestation is to deny our present existence to be eschatological, as belonging to
   the beginning of the time of the End."
5. *Spread the Fire* (January, 1995), p. 18.
6. For the entire report about Heather Harvey, Monica Morgan-Dohner, and
   other children, see Guy Chevreau, *Catch the Fire* (London: HarperCollins,
   1994), pp. 170–75.
7. Report from Melanie Morgan-Dohner in *Catch the Fire*, p. 172.
8. For the complete text, see *Catch the Fire*, pp. 146–49.
9. Dr. John Axler and I are grateful to Magda Zakani, Director of Health
   Records, Bloorview Children's Hospital, for her cooperation and kind assistance.

Chapter Eight: The Kansas City Prophets

1. David Pytches, *Some Said It Thundered: A Personal Encounter with the
   Kansas City Prophets*, 2d ed. (Nashville: Oliver-Nelson, 1991).
2. Ibid., pp. 97–99.
3. Gruen, *Documentation*, pp. 217–21.
4. "Biography for Paul Cain," by Reed Grafke, Associate of Paul Cain Ministries, Charlotte, North Carolina. This was an unpublished, two-page document.
5. Kevin Springer, "Paul Cain: A New Breed of Man," *Equipping the Saints*
   (Fall, 1989), pp. 11–13.
6. The most significant scholarly study of William Branham is C. Douglas
   Weaver, *The Healer-Prophet, William Marrion Branham* (Macon, Ga.: Mercer University Press, 1987).
7. Paul Thigpen, "How Is God Speaking Today?" *Charisma* (September, 1989),
   p. 50.
8. Pytches, *Some Said It Thundered*, p. 18.

Chapter Nine: Prophecy and The Toronto Blessing

1. See Rodney Howard-Browne, *Flowing in the Holy Ghost* (Louisville, Ky.:
   RHBEA Publications, 1993), p. 22.
2. Ibid.
3. Ibid., pp. 22–23.
4. Marc Dupont, as quoted in Guy Chevreau, *Catch the Fire* (London: Harper-
   Collins, 1994), pp. 28–34. My listing of quotations is from a much longer
   text, but I believe I am faithful to the original and am not taking these statements out of context.

5. See Dave Roberts' discussion in *The "Toronto" Blessing* (Eastbourne: Kingsway Publications, 1994), p. 27.

6. Tom Smail, Andrew Walker, and Nigel Wright, *The Love of Power or the Power of Love* (Minneapolis: Bethany, 1994), p. 111.

7. See Wes Campbell's taped message, Toronto Airport Vineyard, October 14, 1994.

8. Larry Randolph, "Renewal and Revival Today," Toronto Airport Vineyard, Friday, November 18, 1994 (audiotape transcript).

9. Larry Randolph, "Pursuing Jesus Before His Gifts," Airport Vineyard (audiotape transcript).

10. See Garry Best and John White, "What is God Doing Today?" October 14, 1994, Toronto Airport Vineyard.

Chapter Ten: Biblical Faith and The Toronto Blessing

1. Timothy White, quoted in James Beverley, *Crisis of Allegiance* (Burlington, Ont.: Welch, 1986), p. 94. White's work was published by Vantage in 1968, but it is now out of print.

2. On Wesley's concerns about the heart, see Thomas C. Oden, *John Wesley's Scriptural Christianity* (Grand Rapids: Zondervan, 1994), pp. 225–26.

3. James D. G. Dunn, *Baptism in the Holy Spirit* (Philadelphia: Westminster, 1970), pp. 225–26.

4. See Daina Doucet, "Ministry Explodes," *Spread the Fire* (March-April 1995), pp. 4–5.

5. The term *reductionism* was suggested by my colleague John Vissers, professor of Systematic Theology, as a way of noting a certain weakness in the theology of the Spirit offered in The Toronto Blessing.

6. See Ryle's comments in Bob Hunter's essay, "The Vineyard Movement: Instruments of Revival or Deception?" (1994), p. 1. This essay is available from Hunter on Internet (hunter44@flexnet.com) or by sending a donation of $7.00 to Bob and Pat Hunter, 135 Marie St., Shelburne, Ontario, Canada, L0N 1S1.

7. J. I. Packer, *Keep in Step with the Spirit* (Old Tappan, N.J.: Revell, 1984), p. 233.

8. Tom Smail, in Smail, Andrew Walker, and Nigel Wright, *The Love of Power or the Power of Love* (Minneapolis: Bethany, 1994), p. 21.

9. Ibid., p. 29.

10. Martin Luther, as quoted in Timothy George, *Theology of the Reformers* (Nashville: Broadman, 1988), p. 314.

Bibliography

Books

Barron, Bruce. *The Health and Wealth Gospel*. Downers Grove, Ill.: Inter-Varsity, 1987.

Bickle, Mike. *Passion for Jesus*. Orlando, Fla.: Creation House, 1993.

Blue, Ken. *Authority to Heal*. Downers Grove, Ill.: InterVarsity, 1987.

Burgess, Stanley M., and Gary B. McGee, ed. *Dictionary of Pentecostal and Charismatic Movements*. Grand Rapids: Zondervan, 1988.

Carson, D. A. *Showing the Spirit: A Theological Exposition of 1 Corinthians 12–14*. Grand Rapids: Baker, 1987.

Chevreau, Guy. *Catch the Fire*. London: HarperCollins, 1994.

Coggins, James R., and Paul Hiebert, eds. *Wonders and the Word*. Winnipeg: Kindred Press, 1989.

Cox, Harvey. *Fire From Heaven*. Reading, Mass.: Addison-Wesley, 1994.

Cross, Edward. *Miracles, Demons, and Spiritual Warfare*. Grand Rapids: Baker, 1990.

Dager, Albert James. *Vengeance Is Ours*. Redmond, Wash.: Sword Publishers, 1990.

DeArteaga, William. *Quenching the Spirit*. Lake Mary, Fla.: Creation House, 1992.

Dixon, Patrick. *Signs of Revival*. Eastbourne: Kingsway, 1994.

Fearon, Mike. *A Breath of Fresh Air*. Eastbourne: Kingsway, 1994.

Gunstone, John. *Signs and Wonders: The Wimber Phenomenon*. London: Daybreak, 1989.

Hamon, Bill. *Prophets and Personal Prophecy*. Shippensberg, Pa.: Destiny Image, 1987.

Hanegraaff, Hank. *Christianity in Crisis*. Eugene, Ore.: Harvest House, 1993.

Harrell, David Edwin, Jr. *All Things Are Possible*. Bloomington: Indiana University Press, 1975.

_____. *Oral Roberts: An American Life*. Bloomington: Indiana University Press, 1985.

Haykin, Michael. *Revivals and Signs and Wonders*. Richmond Hill: Canadian Christian Publications, 1992.

Horton, Michael. *Agony of Deceit*. Chicago: Moody, 1990.

Howard-Browne, Rodney. *Flowing in the Holy Ghost*. Louisville, Ky.: RHEBA Publications, 1993.

_____. *The Touch of God*. Louisville, Ky.: RHEBA Publications, 1992.

Hunt, Dave, and T. A. McMahon. *The Seduction of Christianity*. Eugene, Ore.: Harvest House, 1986.

Hunter, Charles & Frances. *Holy Laughter*. Kingwood, Tex.: Hunter Books, 1994.

Johnian, Mona. *The Fresh Anointing*. Bridge Publishing.

Joyner, Rick. *Visions of the Harvest*. Orlando, Fla.: Creation House, 1988.

Knox, Ronald A. *Enthusiasm*. New York: Oxford University Press, 1961.

Kraft, Charles H. *Christianity With Power*. Ann Arbor, Mich.: Servant Publications, 1989.

Lundy, Daniel G. *Signs and Wonders Today*. Richmond Hill: Canadian Christian Publications, 1992.

MacArthur, John F., Jr. *Charismatic Chaos*. Grand Rapids: Zondervan, 1992.

_____. *Reckless Faith*. Wheaton: Crossway, 1994.

McConnell, D. R. *A Different Gospel*. Peabody, Mass.: Hendrickson, 1988.

McGee, Gary B., ed. *Initial Evidence*. Peabody, Mass.: Hendrickson, 1991.

Moriarity, Michael G. *The New Charismatics*. Grand Rapids: Zondervan, 1992.

Nolen, William A. *Healing: A Doctor in Search of a Miracle*. Greenwich, Conn.: Fawcett Publications, 1974.

Pytches, David. *Some Said It Thundered*. Nashville: Thomas Nelson, 1991.

Roberts, Dave. *The "Toronto" Blessing*. Eastbourne: Kingsway Publications, 1994.

Smail, Tom, Andrew Walker, and Nigel Wright. *The Love of Power or the Power of Love*. Minneapolis: Bethany, 1994.

Smedes, Lewis, ed. *Ministry and the Miraculous*. Pasadena, Calif.: Fuller Theological Seminary, 1987.

Springer, Kevin, ed. *Riding the Third Wave*. Basingstoke, UK: Marshall Pickering, 1987.

Wagner, C. Peter. *The Third Wave of the Holy Spirit*. Ann Arbor, Mich.: Servant Publications, 1988.

Warfield, Benjamin B. *Counterfeit Miracles*. Carlisle, Pa.: The Banner of Truth Trust, 1918.

Weaver, C. Douglas. *The Healer-Prophet, William Marrion Branham*. Macon, Ga.: Mercer University Press, 1987.

White, John. *When the Spirit Comes With Power*. Downers Grove, Ill.: InterVarsity, 1988.

Williams, Don. *Signs, Wonders, and the Kingdom of God: A Biblical Guide for the Reluctant Skeptic*. Ann Arbor, Mich.: Servant Publications, 1989.

Williams, J. Rodman. *Renewal Theology: Systematic Theology from a Charismatic Perspective*. Grand Rapids: Zondervan, 1990.

Wimber, John, and Kevin Springer. *Power Evangelism*. San Francisco: Harper & Row, 1986.

_____. *Power Healing*. San Francisco: Harper & Row, 1987.

_____. *Power Points*. San Francisco: HarperCollins, 1991.

Journal Articles

Cardon, Paul. "'Toronto Blessing' Stirs Worldwide Controversy, Rocks Vineyard Movement." *Christian Research Journal* (Winter, 1995), pp. 5ff.

Cannon, Stephen F. "Kansas City Fellowship Revisited: The Controversy Continues." *The Quarterly Journal* 11 (January-March, 1991), pp. 4, 7–9.

Copestake, David R., and Newton H. Malony. "Adverse Effects of Charismatic Experiences: A Reconsideration." *Journal of Psychology and Christianity* 12 (1993), pp. 245–52.

Farnell, F. David. "The Current Debate About New Testament Prophecy, Part I." *Bibliotheca Sacra* 149 (July-September, 1992), pp. 277–303.

_____. "The Gift of Prophecy in the Old and New Testaments, Part II." *Bibliotheca Sacra* 149 (October-December, 1992), pp. 387–410.

_____. "Does the New Testament Teach Two Prophetic Gifts? Part III." *Bibliotheca Sacra* 150, (January–March, 1993), pp. 62–88.

_____. "When Will the Gift of Prophecy Cease? Part IV." *Bibliotheca Sacra* 150 (April-June, 1993), pp. 171–202.

Ferraiuolo, Perucci, and Paul Carden. "Where Are They Now? A Televangelist Update." *Christian Research Journal* (Fall, 1994), pp. 7–8, 45.

Fisher, G. Richard. "A Look at Spiritual Pandemonium." *The Quarterly Journal: Personal Freedom Outreach* 14 (October-December, 1994), pp. 1f.

Kammer, Donald. "The Perplexing Power of John Wimber's Power Encounters." *Churchman* 106, 1 (1992), pp. 45–64.

Murray, Iain H. "Book Review of Guy Chevreau's *Catch the Fire*." *The Banner of Truth* (March, 1995), pp. 28–29.

Robinson, Thomas A. "The Azusa Street Missions and Its Influential Newsletter." *North American Religion* 1 (1992), pp. 166–68.

Sarles, Ken L. "An Appraisal of the Signs and Wonders Movement." *Bibliotheca Sacra*, 145 (January-March, 1988), pp. 57–82.

Thomas, Robert L. "Prophecy Rediscovered? A Review of *The Gift of Prophecy in the New Testament and Today*." *Bibliotheca Sacra* 149 (January-March, 1992), pp. 83–96.

Wacker, Grant. "Wimber and Wonders—What About Miracles Today?" *Reformed Journal* 37 (April, 1987), pp. 16–19.

Magazine Articles

Author Known

Anderson, Don. "Disquiet in the Tornado." *Canadian Baptist* (March, 1995), pp. 13–14.

Archer, John. "Works of Wisdom & Knowledge." *Charisma* (November, 1992), pp. 31–34.

Backhouse, Norman. "Signs and Wonders." *Prairie Overcomer* (November 1987), pp. 14–17, 29.

Barber, Laurie. "Will We Miss The Blessing?" *Canadian Baptist* (March 1995), pp. 11–12.

Baxter, Ronald E. "Signs and Wonders—Today?" *Evangelical Baptist* (September, 1988), pp. 5–9.

Beverley, James A. "John Wimber, the Vineyard and the Prophets: Listening for a Word from God." *The Canadian Baptist* (March-April, 1992), pp. 32–38.

_____. "Ten Myths About the Toronto Blessing." *The Canadian Baptist* (March 1995), p. 15.

_____. "Beyond Holy Laughter?" *Faith Today* (September-October, 1994), p. 13.

_____. "And Some Should Be Prophets?" *Faith Today* (July-August, 1993), pp. 52–55.

Bickle, Mike. "Administrating Prophecy in the Church." *Equipping the Saints* (Fall, 1989), pp. 23–27.

Birch, Ken. "No Laughing Matter." *The Penecostal Testimony* (February, 1994), p. 27.

Blumhofer, Edith, L. "Dispensing with Scofield." Book Review of *Surprised by the Power of the Spirit*, by Jack Deere. *Christianity Today* (January 10, 1994), pp. 56–57.

Breshears, Gerry. "Encountering the Vineyard." *Third Wave* (April, 1990), pp. 1–23.

Briggs, Roger. "The Gifts of the Spirit and the Ministry of John Wimber." *Fellowship Magazine* (January-February, 1992), pp. 6–8.

Buckingham, Jamie. "Evaluating the New 'Prophecy Movement.'" *Ministries Today* (May-June, 1990), pp. 22–24.

Cain, Paul, and Rick Joyner. "The Clinton Administration: Its Meaning and Our Future." *The Morning Star Prophetic Bulletin* (January, 1993), pp. 1–8.

Capon, John. "Four Books in Search of Toronto." *Baptist Times* (November 10, 1994).

Chantry, Walter. "Powerfully Misleading." *Eternity* (July-August, 1987), pp. 27–29.

Chevreau, Guy. "'Grade A' Fruit." *Faith Today* (March-April, 1995), pp. 26–28.

Corelli, Rae. "Going to the Mat for God." *McLean's* (March 13, 1995), pp. 56–57.

Dean, Robert, Jr. "Don't Be Caught By the Undertow of the Third Wave." *Biblical Perspectives* (May-June, 1990), pp. 1–6.

Dennison, Justin. "The Grapes of Wrath or Blessing?" *Evangelical Baptist* (February, 1995), pp. 20–21; see also p. 25 for his review of *The Love of Power or the Power of Love,* by Tom Smail, Andrew Walker, and Nigel Wright.

Dewey, David. "'Toronto Blessing' Hits Baptist Churches in London." *Baptist Times* (June 30, 1994), p. 2.

Dorsche, Audrey. "A Need for Discernment." *Faith Today* (March-April, 1995), p. 7.

Doucet, Daina. "What Is God Doing in Toronto?" *Charisma* (February, 1995), pp. 20–26.

_____. "Renewal Excites Canadian Churches." *Charisma* (June, 1994), pp. 52–53.

Foster, Richard J. "Who's Misleading Whom in Story on Wimber?" *Eternity* (October, 1987), p. 5.

Gardner, David. "Children and The Toronto Blessing." *Baptist Times* (August 25, 1994), p. 7.

Geddert, Ron. "The Toronto Blessing." *Mennonite Brethren Herald* (October 28, 1994), pp. 2–3.

Gibson, Helen, and Gavin Scott. "Laughing for the Lord." *Time* (August 15, 1994), p. 43.

Grady, Lee. "Resolving Kansas City Prophecy Controversy." *Ministries Today* (September-October, 1990), pp. 49ff.

_____. "Vineyard Revival Spreads Abroad." *Charisma* (September, 1994), p. 74.

_____. "God Can Use Warehouses." *Charisma* (February 1995), p. 4.

Griffin, William A. "We Need God." *Resource* (March-April, 1989), p. 2.

Hardwick, Elizabeth. "Church Going." *The New York Review* (August 18, 1988).

Hill, Clifford. "'Toronto Blessing'—True or False?" *Prophecy Today* (Summer, 1994), pp. 10ff.

Holliday, Richard D. "Spiritual Mediocrity." *Faith Today* (March-April, 1995), pp. 27, 29.

Hough, Robert. "God Is Alive and Well and Saving Souls on Dixon Road." *Toronto Life* (February, 1995), pp. 29–33.

Jensen, Phillip, Tony Payne, et al. "John Wimber, Friend or Foe?" Reprinted from *The Briefing* (April 1990), 40 pages.

Johnson, Gordon H. "Airport Vineyard, Spiritual Gifts." *Evangelical Baptist* (January 1, 1995), pp. 2, 14–15.

Lees, David. "Blow Me Down Jesus." *Saturday Night* (December, 1994), pp. 50–60.

MacNeil, Kirk. "The 'Toronto Blessing': 'A Surprising Work of God' Is a Surprising Conclusion!" *Christian Courier* (March 24, 1995), pp. 11–12.

MacNutt, Judith. "Discerning of Spirits." *Charisma* (November, 1992), pp. 57–60.

MacRae, Andrew D. "The Toronto Blessing: An Experience of Renewal and Revival." *Atlantic Baptist* (February, 1995), pp. 12–13.

Matthews, Larry. "Through a Glass Darkly." *The Canadian Baptist* (March, 1995), p. 7.

Maudlin, Michael G. "Seers in the Heartland." *Christianity Today* (January 14, 1991), pp. 18–22.

Maxwell, Joe. "Is Laughing for the Lord Holy?" *Christianity Today* (October 24, 1994), pp. 78–79.

Morrison, Alan. "How the 'Toronto Blessing' Came to Town." *Evangelical Times* (November, 1994), p. 17.

Nodding, Peter. "Catching the Wind of the Spirit." *Baptist Times* (July 21, 1994), pp. 5, 12.

Ostling, Richard N. "Laughing for the Lord." *Time* (August 15, 1994), p. 43.

Patterson, Robert W. "Review of John F. MacArthur Jr., *Charismatic Chaos; The Gospel According to Jesus;* and *Our Sufficiency in Christ.*" *Christianity Today* (May 18, 1992), pp. 70–75.

Pinnock, Clark. "Can't Tell God How and Where to Work." *The Canadian Baptist* (March, 1995), pp. 9–10.

Reid, Gail. "After the Laughter." *Faith Today* (March-April, 1995), pp. 18–23.

Roberts, Dave. "Rumours of Revival." *Alpha* (July, 1994), pp. 25ff.

Springer, Kevin. "Interview with Paul Cain." *Equipping the Saints* (Fall, 1990), pp. 8–12.

Stackhouse, John G., Jr. "Background to Blessing." *Faith Today* (March-April, 1995), pp. 24–25.

Stafford, Tim. "Testing the Wine from John Wimber's Vineyard." *Christianity Today* (August 8, 1986), pp. 17–22.

Strang, Stephen. "A Caution on Personal Prophecy." *Charisma* (September, 1989), p. 9.

_____. "Floored in Toronto." *Charisma & Christian Life* (February, 1995), p. 106.

Tillen, Tricia. "But Is It a Blessing?" *Christian Herald* (December 3, 1994), p. 8.

Thigpen, Paul. "How Is God Speaking Today?" *Charisma* (September, 1989), pp. 50–56.

Wimber, John. "The Gift of Prophecy." *Charisma* (November, 1992), pp. 53–55.

Witt, Stephan. "The Spirit Shakes a Seeker-Sensitive Church!" *Ministries Today* (November-December, 1994), pp. 22–23.

Woodward, Kenneth L., Jeanne Gordon, Carol Hall, and Barry Brown. "The Giggles Are for God." *Newsweek* (February 20, 1995), p. 54.

Anonymous

"Evangelical Alliance Joint Statement on Toronto Blessing." *Evangelicals Now* (February, 1995), p. 3.

"Healing, Laughter, Falling, Shaking Part of 'Renewal' Sweeping Ontario." *Faith Today* (May-June, 1994), pp. 46–47.

"Kansas City Fellowship Joins Vineyard." *Charisma* (July, 1990), p. 34.

"Toronto Blessing, Evangelical Leaders: It's Not Revival Yet." *Alpha* (March, 1995), p. 36.

"Toronto Blessing Hits Roman Catholic Charismatics." *Baptist Times* (No. 7529, vol. 140), p. 2.

"Truce Called in Bickle Controversy." *Charisma* (September, 1990), p. 42.

"What Happened Next?" *Evangelicals Now* (February, 1995), pp. 1, 8–9.

"Wimber Breaks Silence to Answer Vineyard Critics." *Christianity Today* (March 9, 1992), pp. 66–68.

Newspaper Articles

Author Known

Bennett, Will. "Church Hires 'Holy Bouncers' to Keep Peace." *Independent* (February 27, 1995).

Beverley, James A. "Hardhitting Bestseller Confronts Heresy." *Christian Week* (November 16, 1993). Review of *Christianity in Crisis* by Hank Hanegraaff.

Bickle, Mike. "The True Prophetic Spirit: The Simplicity and Purity of Devotion to Jesus." *Grace City Report, Special Prophetic Edition.* pp. 1ff.

Brown, Andrew. "Churchmen at Odds Over 'Waves of Faith.'" *Independent* (January 25, 1995).

Brown, Barry. "Spiritual Fountain Overflows in Toronto's Vineyard Church." *Buffalo News* (March 4, 1995).

Brown, Mick. "Unzipper Heaven, Lord." *Daily Telegram* (December 3, 1994), pp. 26–29.

Chandler, Russell. "Vineyard Fellowship Finds Groundswell of Followers." *Los Angeles Times* (October 5, 1990).

Conklin, Margery. "Catching the Fire." *Journal Outlook* (November 2, 1994).

Dennison, Justin. "Pastor's Perspective." *Christian Week* (December 13, 1994), p. 15.

DeWitt, Dan. "Signs and Wonders." *St. Petersburg Times* (February 14, 1993).

Eastlick, Jay. "Is God Moving in Society?" *Missourian* (September 17, 1994).

Forward, Brenda. "Mainstream Call to Repentance and Revival." *Baptist Times* (January 24, 1991).

Gillmor, Don. "The Puzzling Case of The Toronto Blessing." *The Globe & Mail* (February 8, 1995).

Gledhill, Ruth. "Ruth Gledhill Experiences the Toronto Phenomena at a Vineyard Church in Putney." *The Times* (June, 1994).

Golden, Rose. "New Wine Poured out at Airport Vineyard." *The Messianic Times* (Spring, 1995), pp. 1, 3.

Goodman, Paul. "The Evangliest Who Is Refreshing Religion." *The Sunday Telegraph* (October 2, 1994), p. 22.

Goodman, Walter. "About Churches, Souls and Show-Biz Methods." *The New York Times* (March 16, 1995), p. C20.

Harpur, Tom. "What the 'Mighty Wind from Toronto' Feels Like." *The Toronto Star* (November 20, 1994), p. E12.

Harvey, Bob. "Toronto Renewal Movement Troubling." *Ottawa Citizen* (October 15, 1994).

_____. "Probing Today's Prophets." *Ottawa Citizen* (March 28, 1992), p. H8.

Hayes, Brian. "Laughing in the Spirit." *The Mail-Star* (February 18, 1995), p. A8.

Hurst, Lynda. "Laughing All the Way to Heaven." *The Toronto Star* (December 3, 1994), pp. A1ff.

Koop, Doug. "Holy Laughing Lifting Spirits." *Christian Week* (March 15, 1994), pp. 1–2.

_____. "Airport Vineyard Still Flying High." *Christian Week* (December 13, 1994), pp. 1ff.

_____. "Emotions Deceive, Warns Pastor." *Christian Week* (December 13, 1994), p. 14.

_____. "'Toronto Blessing' Garnering Worldwide Attention." *Christian Week* (August 23, 1994), pp. 1ff.

Jantz, Harold. "Prayer Rally Links Christians, Lifts Spirits." *Christian Week* (October 18, 1994), pp. 1ff.

_____. "'Toronto Blessing' Is Not the End of the Journey." Editorial, *Christian Week* (February 28, 1995).

Lindsay, James. "Revival Breaks out in London Churches." *England News* (June 17, 1994).

Longley, Clifford. "Toronto Blessing 'Is Mass Hysteria.'" *The Daily Telegraph* (January 28, 1995), p. 8.

McCandlish, James. "Thousands Flock to Church That's Just for Laughs." *National Enquirer* (October 17, 1995).

McPherson, Guy. "Renewal Phenomena and the Wesleyan Tradition." *Christian Info News* (December, 1994).

Newman, Josie. "The Faith Business." *London Free Press* (January 14, 1995).

Paterson, Michael. "Faithful Get High on Holy Spirit." *Scotsman* (1994).

Pinnock, Clark. "Pinnock's Pointers." *Christian Week* (December 13, 1994), p. 15.

Rivenberg, Roy. "A Question of Faith." *Los Angeles Times* (January 28, 1992), pp. E1ff.

Schiller, Bill. "'Blessing' from Metro Church Wins Converts Across Britain." *Toronto Star* (August 25, 1994), pp. 1, 17.

Schwartzberg, Shlomo. "Thank God for Small Miracles." *The Financial Post* (February 25, 1995).

Smyth, Julie. "Pilgrims Worshipping on a Different Plane." *The Globe and Mail* (July 6, 1994).

Stackhouse, John G., Jr. "Encounters at the Vineyard." *Christian Week* (September 20, 1994), p. 17.

Strachan, Eric. "Lining Up to Get Into Church." *The Pembroke Weekend News* (August 20, 1994), p. 5.

Templeton, Darwin. "Church Rocked by 'Blessing' Craze." *Sunday Life* (March 5, 1995), pp. 2–3.

Thompson, Damian. "Roman Catholics Affected by Charismatic Blessing." *Daily Telegraph*.

Vandenakker, Roger. "The Toronto Blessing." *Companions of the Cross* (Winter, 1994), p. 8.

Whittaker, Barry. "Modest Canadians Downplaying 'Blessing.'" *Our Community Press* (January 18, 1995), p. 11.

Woods, Bruce. "Prayers of the Prophets Sound in Hamilton." *Christian Week* (May 11, 1993), p. 2.

_____. "We Say, 'Holy Spirit, Let It Come!'" *Christian Week* (December 13, 1994), p. 20.

Wroe, Martin. "A Drop of the Holy Spirit Has Them Rollin' in the Aisles." *Observer* (September 4, 1994).

Anonymous

"Blessings Abound: The Toronto Blessing, Top Religious Story of 1994." *Christian Week* (January 3, 1995).

"Believers Fall Flat Out for Love of Jesus." *Brisbane Courier Mail* (March 2, 1995).

"Religion Watch." *The Globe and Mail* (September 9, 1994).

"Revival Breaks Out in London Churches."*The Church of England Newspaper* (June 17, 1994), p. 1.

Additional Material

Author Known

Aguirre, Danny. "Some Examples of Holy Laughter in Other Religions." *SCP Newsletter,* 19:2 (Fall, 1994), p. 14.

Alnor, Jackie. "Holy Laughter—Is It Biblical?" *Christian Sentinel* (September, 1994). 11 pages.

Brant, Howard. "Toward an SIM Position on Power Encounter." SIM position paper (n.d.). 24 pages.

Campbell, Ken. "The Mighty Wind from Toronto: A Blessing or a Cursing?" *Liberation* (December, 1994). 3 pages.

Chambers, Joseph R. "Holy Laughter." Part 1. Paw Creek Ministries, Inc. (n.d.). 10 pages.

_____. "Holy Laughter." Part 2. Paw Creek Ministries, Inc. (n.d.). 10 pages.

Cooper, Kristina. "Delusion or the Shock of Real Religion?" *The Tablet* (February 18, 1995), pp. 223–24.

Dager, Albert James. "Latter-Day Prophets. The Restoration of Apostles and Prophets and the Kansas City Vineyard Connection." *Media Spotlight* (special report, n.d.). 32 pages.

_____. "Latter-Day Prophets. The Kansas City Connection." *Media Spotlight* (n.d.). 16 pages.

_____. "Latter-Day Prophets Update. Their Defense Analyzed." *Media Spotlight* (n.d.). 4 pages.

_____. "Holy Laughter—Rodney Howard-Browne and The Toronto Blessing." *Media Spotlight* (1995). 16 pages.

Dupont, Marc. "1994: The Year of the Lion." *Mantle of Praise Ministries*. 4 pages.

_____. "1995: Perspectives." *Mantle of Praise Ministries* (January, 1995). 4 pages.

Fowler, Stanley K. "Signs and Wonders Today: Some Theological Reflections." Reprinted from *Baptist Review of Theology* (Fall, 1993). 6 pages.

Gruen, Ernest. "Documentation of the Aberrant Practices and Teachings of Kansas City Fellowship (Grace Ministries)." Unpublished report (n.d.). 233 pages.

Raycroft, Mary Audrey. "Gifts of the Spirit." Module 2 (n.d.). Study guide from Christian Services Association. 25 pages.

Riss, Richard M. "Azusa Street Manifestation." Unpublished report on Internet (February 9, 1995). 6 pages.

_____. "More on the Revival." Unpublished report on Internet (February 8, 1995). 8 pages.

_____. "History of the 'Laughing Revival.'" Unpublished report on Internet (January 17, 1995). 28 pages.

_____. "The Counterfeit Revival?" Unpublished report (1995). 9 pages.

Smith, Warren. "Holy Laughter or Strong Delusion?" *SCP Newsletter* (Fall, 1994).

Sproule, Wayne. "An Open Letter to Pastor John Arnott and the Brethren in the Ontario Vineyard Churches" (October 17, 1994). 4 pages.

Thomson, Cheryl. "Not Just a Memoir of the Vineyard, 1986–1994." Unpublished paper (February 15, 1995). 24 pages.

_____. "Letter to Concerned Christians" (February 15, 1995).

Tillin, Tricia. "The Toronto Phenomenon: Is It of God?" *Discernment* 5 (July-September, 1994). 4 pages.

Williams, Gordon. "Vineyard Experience." Unpublished paper (n.d.). 11 pages.

Anonymous

Collection of submissions to CETA-Ł Listserv group on Toronto Vineyard Phenomena (September 20–29, 1994). 23 pages.

"Executive Council Report re: Vineyard Movement." *Fellowship Year-book* (1991), pp. 113–14.

"Holy Laughter: Bringing Revival to the Church?" *The 700 Club Fact Sheet* (Virginia Beach: CBN; October 27, 1994). 1 page.

"The Laughing Revival in Canada." *Great News Christian Publication* 7 (October 1994).

"Revival—Has it Come? (Part II)." *The Inkhorn*, published by Amazing Grace Ministries (n.d.). 8 pages.

"Revival Is Unmistakable." *The Herald of His Coming* (December, 1994–February, 1995). 4 pages.

"Statement re: The Signs and Wonders (Vineyard) Movement." Statement of Position of the 1990 Convention of the Fellowship of Evangelical Baptist Churches in Canada (November 8, 1990). 2 pages.

Vineyard Material

Author Known

Campbell, Wes. "Spiritual & Physical Manifestations." Unpublished paper distributed at Pastors and Leaders Meeting, Airport Vineyard renewal services. Toronto (1994).

Chevreau, Guy. "A Map for Renewal." Unpublished paper distributed at Pastors and Leaders Meeting, Airport Vineyard renewal services. Toronto (1994).

_____. "Catch the Fire." Unpublished paper distributed at Pastors and Leaders Meeting, Airport Vineyard renewal services. Toronto (1994).

Deere, Jack. "The Vineyard's Response to *The Briefing*." Vineyard Position Paper #2 (May, 1992). 31 pages.

Dupont, Marc. "A Two-Part Prophecy Concerning Revival Coming to Part of the Church of Toronto." Unpublished paper by Mantle of Praise Ministries, Toronto Airport Vineyard (May 1992 & July 1993).

Grudem, Wayne. "The Vineyard and John Wimber: A More Positive View" (n.d.). 15 pages.

_____. "The Vineyard's Response to *The Standard*." Vineyard Position Paper #3 (June, 1992). 37 pages.

_____. *Power and Truth*. Vineyard Position Paper #4. Anaheim, Calif.: AVC, 1993.

Hunter, Todd. "Board Report." Association of Vineyard Churches (September-October, 1994). 4 pages.

Jackson, Bill. "What in the World is Happening to Us? A Biblical Perspective on Renewal." *Vineyard Campaign* (April, 1994). 18 pages.

Nathan, Rich. "A Response to *Charismatic Chaos*." Vineyard Position Paper #5 (April, 1993). 38 pages.

Perkins, Larry. "Vineyard Presentation to National Fellowship Convention" (November 3, 1990). 9 pages.

Steingard, Jerry. "Preparing for *Revival Fire*." Stratford: Jubilee Vineyard, 1994.

Wimber, John. "Refreshing, Renewal, and Revival." *Vineyard Reflections* (July-August, 1994). 8 pages.

_____. "An Unchanging Destination." *Vineyard Reflections* (September-October, 1994). 6 pages.

_____. "John Wimber Responds to Phenomena." *Vineyard Reflections* (July-August, 1994). 2 pages.

_____. "Why I Respond to Criticism." Vineyard Position Paper #1 (May, 1992). 7 pages.

_____. "John Wimber's Respone to Concerns Regarding the Prophetic." Based on sermons given at the Anaheim VCF (April 28, 1991). 13 pages.

_____. "Where Is God Taking Us As a Movement?" *The Vineyard Newsletter* (Fall, 1988), pp. 1–2.

_____. "Fallen Leaders in the Vineyard: How Should We Treat Them?" (n.d.). 5 pages.

Anonymous

"Discipline Procedures & Pastoral Strategy (Bob Jones)." November 10, 1991.

"Lessons and Tensions When Anointed Leaders Fall." Part I (November 17, 1991); Part II (November 22, 1991).

"Revival Ignites Toronto!" Newsletter from Toronto Airport Vineyard Christian Fellowship (March, 1994). 2 pages.

"Times of Refreshing: An Introduction to the Unique Move of God Experienced in Our Midst Recently." Published by Vineyard Christian Fellowship of San Francisco (May 10, 1994). 2 pages.

"Tips for Praying for People." Unpublished paper from Toronto Airport Vineyard.

Taped and Transcript Messages

Allen, Ron. "From Refreshing to Power Evangelism." Toronto Airport Vineyard (October 13, 1994).

Arnott, John. "Decently and in Order" (n.d.).

_____. "Dynamics of Receiving Spiritual Experiences." Toronto Airport Vineyard (November 18, 1994).

_____. "Receiving the Spirit's Power" (n.d.).

Arnott, John, and Guy Chevreau. Address at Pastors' Conference. Airport Vineyard (October 19, 1994).

Best, Garry, and John White. "What Is God Doing Today?" Toronto Airport Vineyard (October 14, 1994).

Beverley, Jim. "John Wimber and the Prophets: The Debate Over Mike Bickle and the Kansas City Fellowship." Evangelical Theological Society 44th Annual Meeting (San Francisco: November 19–21, 1992).

Bickle, Mike. "Principles for Nurturing the Prophetic Ministry," Toronto Airport Vineyard (January, 1989).

_____. "Prophetic Preparation for Leaders." Metro Vineyard Fellowship (July 24, 1989).

_____. "Public Discipline of Bob Jones" (n.d.).

Cain, Paul. "Paul Cain's Life Testimony" (n.d.).

Campbell, Wes. "Manifestations of the Holy Spirit." Anaheim Vineyard (July, 1994).

_____. "Pastoring the Prophetic." Catch the Fire Conference at Toronto Airport Vineyard (October 13, 1994).

_____. "Spiritual and Physical Manifestations of the Holy Spirit." Toronto Airport Vineyard (October 15, 1994).

Chevreau, Guy. Address at Pastors' Conference. Toronto Airport Vineyard (December 7, 1994).

Clark, Randy. "Let the Fire Fall." Anaheim VCF (July, 1994).

_____. "Catch the Fire." Questions and Answers. Toronto Airport Vineyard (October 14, 1994).

_____. "Evidence of This Present Move." Toronto Airport Vineyard (October 15, 1994).

_____. "Run With the Fire—Anniversary Message." Toronto Airport Vineyard (January 20, 1995).

_____. "Get Out of the Bunkhouse." Toronto Airport Vineyard (January 21, 1995).

Dupont, Marc. "Prayer of the Prophetic." Catch the Fire Conference at Toronto Airport Vineyard (October 13, 1994).

_____. "The Father's Heart and the Prophetic," Toronto Airport Vineyard (November 16, 1994).

_____. "Prophetic School—Part 3." Pastors' Conference. Toronto Airport Vineyard (November 16, 1994).

_____. "Developing a Prophetic Church." Toronto Airport Vineyard (November 18, 1994).

Hanegraaff, Hank. "Counterfeit Revival" (n.d.).

_____. "Bible Answer Man Radio Show." With Tom Stipe (November 29, 1994).

Jennings, Peter. "In the Name of God." ABC Special (March 16, 1995).

Kirby, Jeff. "Jeff and Todd's Most Excellent Adventure." April 17, 1994.

Randolph, Larry. "Renewal and Revival Today." Toronto Airport Vineyard (November 18, 1994).

_____. "Pursuing Jesus Before His Gifts." Toronto Airport Vineyard (November 19, 1994).

Raycroft, Mary Audrey. "Deborah Company." Toronto Airport Vineyard (November 26, 1994).

Riss, Richard. "Handling Objections to Renewal." Toronto Airport Vineyard (March 18, 1995).

Thomas, Larry. "No Laughing Matter." October 10, 1994.

"Toronto Airport Vineyard." *The Fifth Estate*. CBC Television (February 14, 1995).

Readers who wish to interact with the author on the material in this book or who want to share their views and personal experiences can write to:

Dr. James Beverley
Professor of Theology and Ethics
Ontario Theological Seminary
25 Ballyconnor Court
North York, Ont. M2M 4B3
Canada